M: MYSTIQUE OR MISTAKE?
© 2000 by Diane Passno and Focus on the Family. All rights
nternational copyright secured.

Congress Cataloging-in-Publication Data

iane.
ism : mystique or mistake? : rediscovering God's plan for
Diane Passno.
cm.
1-56179-790-1
minism—Religious aspects—Christianity. 2. Women—
s aspects—Christianity. I. Title.

?37 2000
442—dc21   00-032546

n the Family book published by Tyndale House Publishers,
Illinois.

sign: Dave Rhody
oto: ©1999 PhotoDisc, Inc.
lesign: Angela Greenwalt

n the United States of America

03 04 05/10 9 8 7 6 5 4 3 2 1

feminism: mystique or mistake?

rediscovering God's liberating plan for women

femin

mysti
or mist

rediscoverir
liberating
for won

diane pa

TYNDAL
Tyndale House Publisher

FEMIN
Copyri
reserve

Library

Passno,
    Fem
  wome

    ISB
    1.
  Religi

  BT70
  261.8*

A Focus
Wheato

All Scri
NEW A
1963, 1
Founda
HOLY
1973, 1
of Zond
fied NK
Copyrig

No part
or trans
tocopy,

Cover d
Cover p
Interior

Printed

00 01 0

To my daughters and soul mates, Nicole and Danielle;

my wonderful husband, Paul;

And all the extraordinary staff members

at Focus on the Family,

I lovingly dedicate this book.

Table of Contents

Acknowledgments

Throughout the composition of this volume, I have received excellent insight, technical support, and encouragement from a number of people. I can truthfully say that the manuscript would never have been completed without their assistance, godly counsel, and prayers on my behalf. For those readers ... those rare individuals who read the names in the Acknowledgments of books ... you are in for a glimpse at some "modern-day saints"!

For James and Hope Snell ... and the heritage I received as a child!

For Bud and Fern Passno and the heritage my husband, Paul, received as a child!

For Dr. James and Shirley Dobson ... If only the entire world knew what exceptional people you are and just how beautiful, holy, and true is your walk with your Lord!

For Don and Barbara Hodel ... for believing in me more than I believed in myself!

For Janet Parshall, Hank Hanegraaff, and Kay Arthur ... who gave me "just in time" encouragement more than once!

For Steve Reed ... Your vocabulary is worth your attorney fees!

For my partners at Focus ... Tom Mason and Del Tackett ... two very wise men who happen to be pretty funny as well!

For Stan John, Ron Wilson, Paul Hetrick, Jim Weidmann, Yvette Maher, and Kurt Bruner ... Your wisdom, support, and counsel during this project have meant the world to me!

For John Perrodin, Willy Wooten, and Ken Janzen, who made coming to work a joy even when I was struggling with a deadline!

For Craig Osten and Karen Genandt ... Your research files were almost as enlightening as my drawer full of newspaper clippings!

For Bryan Owens and Ernesto "Neto" Segura ... Your computer expertise saved my bacon!

For Dr. Joe Wheeler ... Your letter at the beginning of this project was an inspiration!

For Al Janssen ... What a marvel that we understood each other so well; this book would not have been possible without your keen discernment!

For John Paulk, Mike Haley, Amy Tracy, Shirley Smith, Chris Schweikart, Caia Hoskins, Steve Kipp, Julie Parton, Lissa Johnson, Larry Burtoft, Shawn Daugherty, Lisa Grimes, Gary Barkalow, Susan Long, Leigh O'Dell, Doug Guilzon, Debbie Douglass, Karen Fischer, Dick Sundstrom, and Katy Vorce ... Your insight was invaluable!

For Father Carroll ... Your friendship has been a highlight of my life, and your knowledge of World War II is nothing short of phenomenal!

For Marilyn Johnson and Maeta Goodwin ... my right arms for the last five years!

For Sherri Woods, Mark Maddox, and Larry Weeden ... Your enthusiasm for this project and your unique contributions to getting it off the ground have meant so much to me!

For Pattie Thompson, Connie Kiersted, and JoAnne Thompson ... who have been there faithfully behind the scenes!

And finally to Edie Hutchinson, Jean Stephens, Julie Kuss, Jane Terry, Jeff Masching, and Christina Harrell ... who made this project a reality!

To all of you, my most humble thanks.

Foreword

I had four children, all less than six years old, and each one of them had the chicken pox. The snow was piled up to the bottom of the first-floor windows. And I was tired—bone tired.

When I finally had them all tucked in for the night (or for what I *hoped* would be the night), I turned to the evening news for a view of the world outside my home. But I found no comfort there. Shrill, pointed voices were challenging the women of America to discover their self-worth. Those voices told us to march under the shibboleth, or banner, of "self-actualization."

Subtle but profound shifts in the advertisements from Madison Avenue were redefining women—images built on the message of modern American feminism. Now, instead of an apron and a house-dress, Mom wore a three-piece suit, carried a briefcase, and threw some unidentifiable object in the toaster as she ran out the door. She would find *true* happiness only if she worked outside the home.

The feminists had been telling us for some time (as they certainly had captured the attention of the major media in this country) that motherhood was an illegitimate profession. They questioned the concept of marriage and stated that this institution needed redefining—a breaking away from traditional gender roles.

Gender roles? What were those? I had fallen madly in love with my high school sweetheart and wanted to spend the rest of my life with him. I remember on my wedding day how feminism manifested itself in a rather direct way. I was looking into the face of my beloved and started saying my vows. I promised to love, honor, and—then it happened. Just as I said, "obey," the woman who was about to become my sister-in-law (and who was already a feminist) cleared her voice in such a piercing way that I am sure the people in the next town heard her. This was her way of registering her opinion on women and their role in a marriage. The irony was that *she* was not promising to obey. I was, and it was my choice. Wasn't that what feminism was supposed to be all about?

That word *choice* took on a deadly meaning during those precious pre-school years for my children. My first baby was born just after the *Roe v. Wade* decision was handed down by the United States Supreme Court. But while the major media carried all the feminist diatribes on "choice," no one reminded women of what they had known intuitively since the beginning of time—how much a woman can fall in love with motherhood. No one prepares you for the depth of feeling and commitment you have for these precious gifts from heaven. And yet, in the marketplace of ideas, women were talking about choosing to take the lives of their pre-born children. They said it was their body, their choice.

But that didn't even make sense. I remember so clearly how there was no question during my pregnancies that two people were bound together. I could be sleeping while the baby was awake. I could be still and the baby had the hiccups. I had hazel eyes and my first-born had blue eyes. My body? My body was the place where a miracle was taking place. I never felt more like a woman than when I was pregnant.

I lived in a state where many of the founding women of modern feminism resided, so I heard a steady stream of their apologetic for a feminist worldview. I still remember so clearly one of the overarching themes of their manifesto—women as victims. Somehow, being born a woman had put me in a lower category of human beings. I was second-class, second-best, second-place, or so I was told. But I didn't feel that way.

I loved being a woman, and still do, even as I approach middle age. When my daughters were born, we certainly didn't send out announcements saying, "Good news! We have a new baby victim."

I took my definition from a higher source. I knew that God, in His infinite wisdom, had created me as a woman purposely. He had a custom designed plan for my life and part of His purpose was to make me female. I did not consider that fashioning to be a deficit, but rather the reflection of His imprint on my life. Why? Because in Him "we live and move and have our being" (Acts 17:28). I am defined ultimately not by my sex but by my being. I am His and He is mine. That is where I get my self-worth—knowing *whose* I am.

When I finally turned off the television that winter night, I tiptoed into the bedrooms of my sleeping children. I listened to their steady, even breathing. I bent down and felt their brows, now grown less feverish and I tried to burn their sweet baby fragrance into my memory. As I tucked the blankets carefully under their chins, I cried— not tears of sorrow, but tears of real joy. I thanked God for making me a woman, a wife, and a mother.

Rather than listening to the roar of the culture, I was listening to the still, small voice of the One who loved me unconditionally. He had plans for my welfare and He gently asked me to wait on Him. These little ones would soon be grown (that is the bittersweet part of mothering) and there was a whole world of opportunities that He was preparing for me, in His perfect time.

I am a woman, and God has a place for me in His work. I now have the privilege of talking to thousands of people daily through a radio show that goes all over the country. I continuously hear from women who have been caught in a web of deception that the feminist movement has thrown out over this nation.

When Diane Passno shared with me the stirring in her heart to write this book, I felt my heart leap. Like her, I know that women have been lied to. I hear it every day. And, like her, I know that women have been hurt as a result of this movement. (For example, I get an overflow of calls when we do programs on post-abortion pain.) I could not wait for Diane to start writing so that more women would be spared the heartache of this grand illusion.

Diane truly cares for women and she knows the emptiness this radical ideology has fostered. With true compassion, she walks us through the history of a movement that in truth is not about women and freedom, but brokenness and bondage.

Diane, thank you for so lovingly doing what needed to be done for the sake of women. You have exposed the feminist mystique for what it truly is—a terrible mistake.

Janet Parshall
Wife, mother, and thankful to be a woman
Washington, D.C.

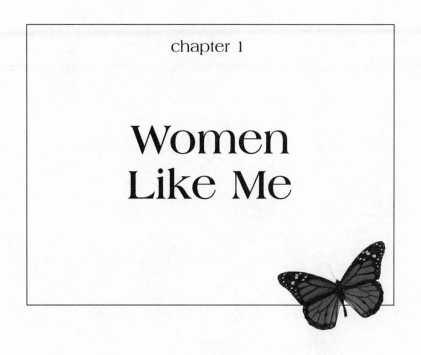

chapter 1

Women
Like Me

We've been duped.

An entire generation of women.

We bought a lie that sounded so good when it came from the mouths of sophisticated, educated, articulate women. Women we wanted to be like. Women who could verbalize the things that we couldn't.

- Equal pay for equal work? Of course! That's only fair!
- More opportunities for women in the workplace? Of course! Women have wonderful gifts and abilities!
- Encouragement for men to be more civilized and understanding of our gender? Of course! Both sexes benefit!
- The opportunity for women to openly support one another in a movement whose time has come? Of course! Who wouldn't want to be part of something so exciting ... so empowering?

So what happened?

It is the beginning of a new century, and the feminist movement has lost its razzle-dazzle. The very women who bought into this agenda wholeheartedly thirty years ago are now assessing the results. And these are the questions we are asking individually:

- Why don't I resonate today with the spokeswomen for the National Organization for Women (NOW) when they are interviewed on television?
- Why doesn't anyone I know belong to that organization?

3

- Why do I feel depressed and defensive when I see how women are portrayed in movies?
- Why does my personal morality feel out of place in the culture in which I live?
- Why does living out the feminist blueprint for personal happiness seem to be destroying the young adults I know?
- Why is my Christian worldview about sexuality and gender roles mocked by the entertainment world?
- Why do I get tongue-tied and feel guilty when I'm talking about my morality with someone who is really "with it" and doesn't understand my feelings?
- Why do feminists hate men when most of the men in my life are not jerks, but really good people?

At one time in my life, I called myself a feminist. I have followed the feminist movement since college. But over the years, I have become increasingly disenchanted with the feminist spokeswomen and their agenda. About twenty years ago, I started tearing out newspaper and magazine clippings that made me angry about the movement … things I wanted to write to the editor about but just didn't take the time. When that stack of articles filled a file drawer, I jokingly commented to some of my professional peers that I was mad enough about the negative impact of the movement on our culture to write a book! And this volume is a result of their challenge to me to do so … to put into words the betrayal that women like me are feeling.

Women like me. What does that describe? I am a committed Christian, but in some ways, my faith has nothing to do with the disappointment I feel about feminism. A non-Christian could have some of the same complaints as I do. I am happily married and deeply respect my spouse, but my marital status also has little to do with my sense of deception, as a single woman would have many of my same concerns. I am well educated and well read. I am enjoying a successful career, but at one point in my life, when my children were young, I was a homemaker. I would describe myself as quite liberated. I would probably be someone whom the feminists would love to have in their club. So why am I not a dues-paying member of NOW?

I was first introduced to feminism in the late 1960s and early 1970s while I was a student at UCLA. This was an incredibly historic time to be in college because a monumental shift in cultural values was occurring right in front of our eyes! The older generation "didn't get it," but the younger generation gobbled it up like candy. Students had a choice of which campus event to attend: a "burn your bra" bonfire or a Vietnam war protest, a hippie gathering in a coffee house or a frat party where the beer flowed and all the athletes went a little crazy. Young men on campus were partying while their friends and classmates were being killed in the jungles of Vietnam in a war that nobody quite understood.

Campuses were segmented by groups: the old guard, which still belonged to the fraternity/sorority crowd; and the new guard, which touted free everything—free love, free drugs, and "free thought." Everyone was riding some kind of wave, and for twenty-year-olds living away from home for the first time, the choices available to them were mind-boggling.

All the women on my campus considered themselves feminists, even the most conservative. The same laughing young women who were burning their bras were flirting with the fraternity men who conducted panty raids in the dorms after the lights went out. There was no perceived disconnect between the feminist ideology that was becoming popular and what the majority of women were actually doing ... getting married and having babies just as their mothers and grandmothers had done.

I also considered myself a feminist and began to follow what the spokeswomen of the movement were saying. I bought into much of what was being preached and carried their philosophies to the workplace when I got my first job as a social worker. I was proud of the accomplishments of feminists who were fighting the battles for equal pay for equal work, since I was a direct beneficiary financially! I was ecstatic about the emerging career and sports opportunities that would be available for future generations of women.

When I left the workplace in 1975 to have babies, the Equal Rights Amendment was receiving a lot of publicity, and I followed the discussion on talk radio and in the newspaper. The proposed language of the amendment was so simple, and it was supported politically by women such as First Lady Betty Ford, Maureen Reagan, daughter of a president, and even "Dear Abby," Abigail Van Buren![1]

Why was there such debate associated with it when these women were so "likeable"? And why did the detractors, when interviewed on the news, make so much sense? Would this amendment, if ratified by the states, really force women into military combat? Would absentee fathers be "off the hook" when it came to paying child support, as a result of the legislation? Would rape no longer be a punishable offense if the amendment were passed? Would we have to use unisex bathrooms? Why did our feminist spokeswomen want it so badly if it would really hurt women rather than help them? These questions began to chisel away at my blind faith in the movement, and I began to question everything I read.

During the time that I was a homemaker with young children, one of the activities I looked forward to with anticipation was a bimonthly meeting of the mothers involved in a church preschool that both of my daughters attended. The mothers would gather together to talk about their kids, share recipes, discuss books, and thoroughly enjoy the opportunity to have adult dialogue in a space of time carved out of lives consumed with diapers, crayons, and baby talk. On occasion, we were able to hear lectures from different organizations in the community, and on one such morning, two guests from NOW addressed the group. The visit is as vivid to me today as if it had happened only this week, when in reality, it occurred over twenty years ago.

I particularly remember what a resounding disappointment the two women were, not only to me, but to the other mothers present as well. Our guests could best be described as young and immature. The focal point of their message was that the male population was the antagonist and enemy of every living female. Neither woman could articulately answer my questions about the Equal Rights Amendment, although this was a front-page news story at the time. On my way home, I thought, *NOW needs to do a better job of representing themselves if they ever expect to get the support of women like me. They can't even address the basics. What do they think we are ... mindless ninnies?*

Many years have passed since that meeting, my daughters are grown, and my husband and I have an empty nest. Our house is quiet in the morning; the sounds of young children no longer wake us. However, some things don't change, and my opinion of NOW has remained the same these past two decades. The organization has never appealed to me nor my peers, despite our various ways of looking at the world and culture. I have felt a keen disappointment in the feminists of my generation, whose main message has been one of embracing reproductive freedom, the lesbian lifestyle, and a self-centered "victim" philosophy that is not only tiresome, but self-defeating. Their claim to a membership of one-half million represents less than one-half of 1 percent of women in the United States today.[2]

NOW and well-recognized feminists have orchestrated efforts in universities and the media, as well as the advertising industry, that should have indoctrinated an entire generation of women. Yet the movement doesn't have the numbers to support its claims to success. The majority of women in this country do not align themselves with the message or the angry, brow-beating, outspoken women who deliver it. The feminists of the earlier half of the century who fought for the rights of women to vote and to hold equal employment won battles that needed to be fought ... battles about which all women could agree and could be like-minded combatants. However, the feminists of the current generation have an agenda that is very divisive in nature, and the majority of women simply are not getting on the bandwagon and yelling "tallyho" to support it.

Why has their message failed? I've been privileged to be able to talk and listen to literally thousands of women over the years, both professionally as a social worker in Los Angeles County, and later in administrative positions at Focus on the Family. I've listened to women from all social, economic, and cultural levels. I was also an avid volunteer when I was a homemaker, and learned firsthand how women "behind the scenes" can impact institutions and culture. It's my desire that the ones who read this book will breathe a collective sigh of relief for the comfort of knowing that there are others out there who also feel "a little out of sync" with Hollywood and the feminists featured in news magazines and newspapers.

I should state that I am writing this from a Christian worldview. You may or may not embrace that ideology. Regardless, I hope I will be able to help each of you come to grips with some of the discomfort you feel with feminism. If you are a Christian, I hope you will be able to comprehend more clearly how gender roles are framed scripturally. I also hope to help you understand why feminism is bankrupt as a movement ... why it has become meaningless to thinking women today. Christian women have a message to tell the world about true liberation, the wonderful way in which the Lord views our gender. And we need to be the articulate instigators for change in our culture rather than bumbling reactors.

Many of my responsibilities at Focus on the Family impact our relationships with our constituents; for example, mail, phone contacts, and distribution of resources. Other responsibilities affect our staff; for example, human resource issues. I deal with many "nuts and bolts" matters within the organization, areas that have always been my passion! I speak quite frequently within the walls of Focus, but I think I communicate better in writing.

I needed the exercise in recording the thoughts in this book as much as any of you who are reading these words, even though I have probably paid more attention to the feminist movement over the years than most women. If Christian women want to impact culture, they need to be prepared to dialogue with anyone who crosses their path: "Always being ready to make a defense to everyone who asks you to give an account for the hope that is in you" (1 Peter 3:15).

Why is feminism a worldview that is totally contradictory to a Christian worldview? Why is it so "uncomfortable" for so many of us to accept what feminists have to say? Can the movement be turned around? Why do young women in their twenties, who have been molded in a culture framed by feminists, have difficulty understanding and accepting the incredible role the Lord has outlined for women scripturally?

My desire is to help women of all ages learn to grasp the important "talking points" of the debate so that we can be prepared to refute those things that actually hurt women rather than help them. No woman wants to play the part of one of the *Stepford Wives*, a movie about women whose husbands replaced them with robots. But neither should we be the robots that the feminists want us to be, accepting their definition of our roles without question. Let us examine the feminist movement together by beginning with a brief, eye-opening history lesson.

chapter 2

Frances: A Wonderful Beginning

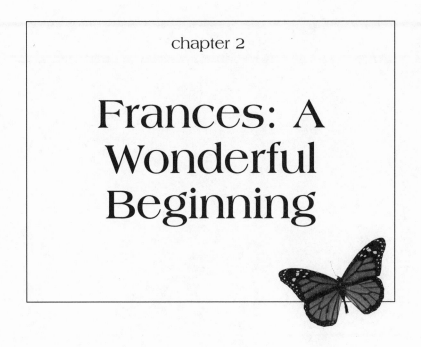

Does anyone still recognize the name of Frances Willard? Does her name ring with "feminism" in the same way as Betty Friedan or Gloria Steinem? Look it up in an encyclopedia or history book, and you get a single paragraph. Lost is the account of the impact this woman had on our culture in the late 1800s.

If you visit Statuary Hall in the Capitol in Washington, D.C., you will see that every state is represented by two marble statues of its most honored citizens. There are a few women among the 100 statues. Illinois chose Frances Willard for this incredible honor. At the time of her death, over a century ago in 1898, more than 30,000 persons filed by her casket in one day. News coverage of her death stated that "no woman's name is better known in the English speaking world than that of Miss Willard, save that of England's great queen." Edward Wheeler of the *Literary Digest* wrote, "She was an awakener of women to the possibilities of true womanhood and she has probably done more than any other person who ever lived to bring to those of her own sex the world over, an adequate realization of their own powers."[1]

Frances was the first president of the women's college within Northwestern University when a "women's crusade" shook the Midwest in 1873-74. Dr. Dana Robert of the Boston University School of Theology describes what occurred:

> In Hillsboro, Ohio, in December of 1873, a group of
> Protestant church women went to hear a temperance
> speaker. The women became so excited by the dangers of

liquor portrayed in the speech that they stormed the local
saloon with prayer and non-violent protest. Across the
Midwest, normally quiet housewives began to march and
to accost druggists, hotel owners, and saloon keepers and
demand that they refuse to sell liquor. Women dropped to
their knees for pray-ins at local saloons and refused to leave
until the saloons shut down. Within three months, the
women had driven liquor out of 250 villages and towns.
Opened casks of liquor were poured down the streets. By
the end of the Women's Crusade, over 900 communities in
31 states and territories had experienced it. Nationwide,
750 breweries were closed. Thousands of women felt
empowered by the crusade, which was the first time many
of them had taken a public stand for anything.[2]

Willard was strongly impacted by this crusade, although she
was not an actual participant. She became very active in the
Women's Christian Temperance Union (WCTU) when it was
founded shortly thereafter, and became its president in 1879. In
order to understand the importance that this organization held for
women in the 1800s, it's necessary to understand the cultural context. Women were powerless. They could not vote. In the majority
of states, their identity was subsumed to their husband's. They had
no legal rights; they could not own property, nor could they have
custody of their children in case of divorce.

Prosecution for wife abuse and rape was rare, and the state-
regulated "age of consent" was as low as seven for children in one
state, thereby allowing child prostitution to flourish in some areas.[3]
Men had no legal obligation to support their wives or children.
Alcoholism was a major problem. Dr. Robert states further that in
1900, one in every 116 Americans was employed by the liquor
industry.[4] This was as serious an issue for women in that century as
drug addiction is for our culture.

Willard's interest in Prohibition was personal. Her brother was an alcoholic, and both his sons became alcoholics as well. However, during her tenure as president, the WCTU did not restrict itself to this single issue. Women's suffrage was key to the movement. Willard also campaigned for prostitution laws that would make the "customer" as guilty as the prostitute. Willard helped establish homes where prostitutes could stay until they found another way to make a living. On the subject of rape, Willard wrote,

> It is by holding men to the same standard of morality that society shall rise to higher levels, and by punishing with extreme penalties such men as inflict upon women atrocities compared with which death would be infinitely welcome. When we reflect that in Massachusetts and Vermont it is a greater crime to steal a cow than to abduct and rape a girl, and that in Illinois rape is not considered a crime, it is a marvel not to be explained that we go the even tenor of our way, too delicate, too refined, too prudish to make any allusion to these awful facts, much less take up arms against these awful crimes. We have been the victims of conventional cowardice too long.[5]

Willard had her hand in "every pot." So many of her ideas were revolutionary at the time, yet we take them for granted now. The WCTU was able to circulate a petition internationally and obtain eight million signatures urging governments to stop the traffic of opium and other drugs.[6] The members lobbied the fashion industry to get rid of corsets that were causing health problems for women. The WCTU promoted sports for women, and Willard took up bicycling, which had been "off limits" to her gender. Willard's prison work was revolutionary. She proposed separate quarters for men and women, as well as female prison matrons to care for female prisoners.

And in all of these efforts, the spiritual message of the WCTU was never neglected. Bible studies were conducted in every setting, be it prisons, lumber camps, or the homes of former prostitutes. Willard wrote, "These make an aggregate of several thousands of women who are regularly studying and expounding God's word to the multitude, to say nothing of the army in home and foreign missions, who are engaged in church evangelism."[7]

Willard's position on equal opportunities for women was beautifully stated in a speech she gave in Washington, D.C., in 1891:

> It is the unanimous voice of the Council that all institutions of learning and of professional instruction, including schools of theology, law, and medicine, should, in the interests of humanity, be as freely opened to women as to men; that opportunities for industrial training should be as generally and as liberally provided for one sex as for the other, and the representatives of organized womanhood in this Council will steadily demand that in all avocations in which both men and women engage, equal wages shall be paid for equal work; and, finally, that an enlightened society should demand, as the only adequate expression of the high civilization which it is its office to establish and maintain, an identical standard of personal purity and morality for men and women.[8]

It is obvious that Frances Willard was a major champion of women's rights and a powerful reformer of society. So why is she a stranger to women of our time? Many historians feel there were two reasons her name faded from history. The first was because the Prohibition movement became "laughable" in later years, especially when the legislation enacted to outlaw liquor was repealed. Also,

Carry Nation is the name most associated with temperance. The second reason, and I feel the deciding factor, was the straightforward Christian framework of the WCTU. Everything Willard did in her remarkable life was based on her understanding of Scripture.

In her last known interview, Frances Willard recounted how she had accepted Jesus Christ as her Lord and Savior: "I remembered the evening when in the old church at home I heard the invitation for those who would confess Christ to come forward and kneel at the altar. . . . I went straight to that altar without looking to the right or left, and though trembling so that I could feel my heart beat as I went forward, I was saying to myself, 'He that confesseth me before men, him will I confess before my Father and the holy angels.'"[9] In that same interview, she stated,

> I have had man's increment to the Scriptures so
> much, that I now don't think much of it. I have gone
> back literally to the simple gospel. I believe that if it
> should be lived just one day, the world would pass from
> death unto life. . . . I do not pretend to have attained, but
> I have at least got the concept of what the New
> Testament is for. It seems to me to be the world's text
> book of the theory and practice of being a man and a
> brother.[10]

It would be naïve to say that every member of the WCTU during Willard's lifetime shared her Christian faith and her passion for evangelism. The agenda of the WCTU was radical, and women jumped on board because of its message, "Do Everything." The message was one of freedom for a class that had been suppressed for too long. However, Willard's message was based on practical Christian principles, and although she addressed inequities in the workplace, she also was an advocate of women who stayed at home as wives and mothers. Some say her most inspiring speeches were about "home protection" and the initiation of laws that protected women in their role as homemakers.

The consensus of many scholars is that Willard is not a heroine to twenty-first-century feminists because of secularization of the movement. Current feminists feel the Church is a patriarchal institution that has outlived its role in culture. Their agenda is directly contrary to the teachings of the Church. Willard would not have agreed with this philosophy: Her passion for reform existed in perfect harmony with traditional interpretation of Scripture.

The Church has always played such a strong role in our culture. How did feminists supersede that role and the traditional teaching of the Church in their quest for "rights"? It is my feeling that they would never have won the minds and loyalty of women if the Church had addressed women's concerns from the start. Feminism could so easily have been a Christian movement within the structure of the Church because it had everything to do with human dignity.

Why wasn't it? Was male leadership so entrenched in denominations that it couldn't see or understand the issues? Willard was a diehard Methodist. She spoke on temperance in Methodist churches and spearheaded many of the social movements that church members supported and in which they participated. However, she was not allowed "as a woman" to attend the general conference of the denomination even though she and a handful of other women were elected by their congregations to do so.[11]

Women involved in the civil rights battle early in the movement had credibility because their issues concerned *every* woman. Susan B. Anthony's name will forever be linked to women's suffrage. What an uphill battle she fought! In 1868, Congress adopted the Fourteenth Amendment to the Constitution, the first to define "citizen" and "voters" as male. Anthony was arrested in 1872 for voting illegally in the presidential election. It took another six years for the Susan B. Anthony Amendment, granting women the right to vote, to be introduced in the United States Congress, and an additional 42 years for the Nineteenth Amendment to the Constitution to be ratified. Was this initiative to grant over half the population the right to participate in the electoral process a result of a Christian movement? No . . . it happened outside of the Church.

Other notable women followed Willard and Anthony: Clara Barton, who organized the American Association of the Red Cross; Ann Sullivan, who altered the meaning of the word *handicapped* forever when she taught Helen Keller to speak; and Rosa Parks, who made an incredible stance on a public bus that sparked the first of the great civil rights protests in 1955. These women were responsible for remarkable contributions because they offered meaningful solutions to very painful and unfair situations. If you were a battered woman or had been raped and were pregnant, the WCTU and, a century later, NOW, became platforms through which those hurts and anger could be channeled and through which legislation was enacted. If you performed an employment task that was the same as the man standing next to you in the assembly line, but were paid much less because of your gender, these women's groups offered hope and justice.

The organized Church had every conceivable reason to be involved in these areas as well, but was not. Because of confusion over the role of women scripturally in marriage as well as in the workplace, the pulpit was not in sync with the reality of women's lives . . . their concerns, their areas of giftedness, their ability to contribute to the Church and society in ways other than teaching Sunday school.

It is my opinion that the Church woke up too late to stop the secular women's movement from impacting culture, and parachurch organizations are still playing catch up. If Christian leaders had stepped in to protest discrimination in employment in a significant way early on, women would have supported that effort, and organizations like the WCTU and NOW would not have been needed to fill the void. The problem continues in many denominations today: Biblical teaching and principles are disassociated from the social issues we all wrestle with when we leave the sanctuary. There is a disconnect.

For example, thirty years ago when pregnancies occurred out of wedlock, churches were well prepared to discuss with the woman the consequences of unscriptural behavior, but Christian crisis pregnancy centers did not exist then. Where did those women go for help? When the Supreme Court decision of *Roe v. Wade* was handed down in 1973 legalizing abortion, the Planned Parenthood clinic down the street was a convenient option for women, particularly when abortion was presented in such a rational way ... as a woman's right.

If you were unmarried and had gone too far in a sexual relationship with your boyfriend, Planned Parenthood was a friend that didn't question your morals, that didn't hold you to personal accountability for the decisions you'd made, and that would help you out of the jam with quiet confidentiality. You didn't really want to bear the shame involved in going to the church to hear that you had sinned and that you would have to assume responsibility for the predicament you were in. The abortion clinic didn't make any judgements about sexual immorality, and better yet, it got rid of the "problem" quietly without anyone else knowing about it. This was very convenient for the boyfriend as well; he never had to assume any responsibility for the child or for his sexual behavior.

Where was the Christian alternative? Where was the Christian option for a woman in trouble and in pain? To this day, even the Christian crisis pregnancy centers are, for the most part, operated outside of denominations.

How did a social movement that began under the title of the Women's *Christian* Temperance Union, founded by Christian women grounded in Scripture, get so mangled 100 years later? How did a women's movement that preached social justice, established on

Christian principles, become a movement that mocks those same principles today? How could a movement that stressed moral purity for *both* sexes become a movement that preaches sexual freedom with no restraint, lesbian rights, and a hatred for the male gender?

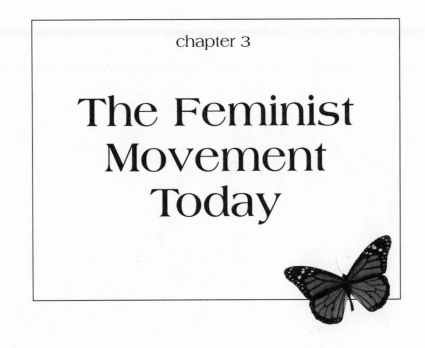

chapter 3

The Feminist Movement Today

The actress Goldie Hawn is everybody's "sweetheart." She's adorable, articulate, and as beautiful now in her fifties as she was when we all fell in love with her in her twenties. If I were to ask a roomful of women the names of prominent feminists of our generation, her name would not be one of them. She is in a special category we reserve for people we like: She's an actress who is enjoyable to watch on the screen, a good mom, and she seems to make sense when any magazine does a cover article on her. I would be hard pressed to find anyone with a particularly negative feeling about Goldie.

Now I want you to take the mental image of beautiful, loveable Goldie, and compare that to these quotes from recent articles in a well-known publication. In response to a question regarding men and infidelity, Goldie responded, "They all cheat."[1] Another question regarding happiness: "I want to know where joy lives. . . . I'd interview scientists, religious leaders, and heads of state. I want to find out exactly what it is that makes people happy. I want to look into the biology, the chemistry of the human brain, and try to find new ways to access a level of happiness within us."[2] On marriage: "It has to do with freedom. . . . I'm not trapped in my relationship. . . . We're individuals who, every day of our lives, wake up and choose to be together. That's a very different dynamic. It's empowering."[3]

Talking about marriage two years earlier, she said, "I don't like fusion. I think it's dangerous. You lose personal power."[4] (Goldie is not married to Kurt Russell, whom she has lived with for more than twenty years. They have raised three children.) On being born female: "I think women have to go very deep down and get to the core of what it is to be female ... because that is power. That is a power given to us at birth ... the mother hands down female power to her daughter."[5]

These quotes could be dissected in depth. But if we were to summarize them quickly, we could assume that all men are unfaithful to their spouses or girlfriends; that joy is something manufactured by the human brain and has nothing to do with a relationship to God or service to others; that marriage is an unnecessary institution; and that genetically, females are granted special power just because they are born women and not men. Each statement reflects the twenty-first-century feminist agenda and is totally alienated from the tenets of Christianity. Sadly, it is the thinking of the majority of our cultural mouthpieces today. This is called a postmodern interpretation of reality.

Postmodernists think all values are relative; what may be true for you may not be true for me, and morality is an individual's choice. The concept of an absolutely moral, sovereign God is "old think," and those who believe in absolute Truth are perceived as oppressive or intolerant. "Do your own thing as long as you don't hurt anybody" is the rule of the game and the "object" of the game of life is to "be happy." This has become the motto, the raison d'être, for an entire generation; careers, marriages, and relationships survive only as long as the people involved are "happy" and "fulfilled."

There is a problem with this line of thinking. The late Dr. Francis Schaeffer wrote in his classic book *How Should We Then Live?*,

> If there is no absolute moral standard, then one cannot say in a final sense that anything is right or wrong. By absolute we mean that which always applies [to all people], that which provides a final or ultimate standard. There must be an absolute if there are to be morals, and there must be an absolute if there are to be real values. If there is

no absolute beyond man's ideas, then there is no final appeal to judge between groups whose moral judgements conflict. We are merely left with conflicting opinions.[6]

The secular feminist agenda thrives in a postmodern culture, since the movement is basically selfish or self-centered in nature. It's all about women and what they want, and has nothing to do with what is healthy for all members of the culture. Feminism rejects the existence of a true God who knows what is best for His creation and who lays out clear principles in Scripture by which His creation is to live.

How did feminism evolve from a Christian movement to a postmodern one? Just as the Church failed to create meaningful social initiatives that would mitigate the serious injustices that were plaguing women at the beginning of the twentieth century, our government contributed to the unraveling of the homemaker role just prior to World War II. During the years of the Great Depression (1929-1938), the government intervened with social programs that were designed to alleviate the impact of the devastating economic recession. These programs, in essence, removed social responsibility from the Church and transferred it to the State.

In 1937, when there was a serious stock market decline, including massive labor strikes, the United States Supreme Court ruled in favor of a minimum wage law for women. A few years later, when women went to work en masse to support the war effort, their traditional "stay at home and raise the children" roles began to unravel.

Despite their contributions to the war effort, however, in the years following World War II, the culture did not offer career choices to women who were in the workforce. There were really only three "professional" fields that women of my generation (those in college in the late 1950s and early 1960s) usually pursued. Those areas were nursing, teaching, and office support. If college was not an option, women could be waitresses, factory workers, or do domestic and custodial work. Homemakers were treated as if they had checked their brains at the door. Women in any professional role were not respected as being equal to men in any endeavor outside of the home.

More women were attending college than at any time in our country's history in the 1960s. However, opportunities to use that education were limited, even if the course of study and degree were the same as those obtained by male students. I am aware of only one woman in my graduating class from a large suburban high school who became an attorney rather than a secretary. Women pilots on commercial air carriers? Extremely rare. Female students in medical school? A small percentage. Female stockbrokers? Not many. Those of you in your fifties or older understand the reality of what our limitations were professionally. And those of you in your twenties may find all of this very difficult to believe since the doors are wide open to you professionally.

It wasn't until the publication of Betty Friedan's classic missive *The Feminine Mystique* in 1963 that the feminist movement experienced visible revitalization, and the response to women's issues became completely secularized. Again, at the risk of sounding repetitive, in so many ways this is tragic because Frances Willard had been both a serious Christian as well as the most respected voice of the women's social justice movement in the late nineteenth century. The Church had every opportunity to grasp the movement that she articulated, but it did not. The government and NOW took over.

Instead of continuing to focus on gains in those areas that were benefiting women of all races and economic levels, the feminist movement made a weird turn in the 1970s, the era of legalized abortion and the proposed Equal Rights Amendment. By then, all pretense of a women's movement based on Christian principles was gone. Outspoken feminists began to tout the philosophy that there were no differences at all between men and women, except those physical characteristics associated with reproduction (how inconvenient!). We have had to endure a period of history in which the genetic differences between the sexes have been ignored in the name of "equality" so women could become more man-like and men could become more woman-like.

Feminists and their cohorts in psychology and education brainwashed an entire generation into thinking that the sexes were no different, and that the culture needed to change the way it looked at males and females. Gloria Steinem said in an interview, "We've had a lot of people in this country who have had the courage to raise their daughters more like their sons. Which is great because it means they're more equal. . . . But there are many fewer people who have had the courage to raise their sons more like their daughters. And that's what needs to be done."[7]

Is it any wonder that this type of nonsense has resulted in male/female gender confusion with tragic consequences? The impact on dating alone for single women has been disastrous. (We will discuss that at length in an ensuing chapter.) Again, the pulpit had an incredible opportunity to provide women who were facing these confusing cultural signals with a wonderful message: God intentionally created uniqueness in design between men and women, and each gender is absolutely essential to culture *because* of its differences. Perhaps this was preached from some pulpits, but the culture and the entertainment industry had a more visible platform than the church, so God's message has not been heard by an entire generation of women.

The problem with a postmodern worldview is that ultimately, the person or the movement with the most power imposes its viewpoint on everyone else. Since the Church has been quiet on the issue, or has subordinated itself to the movement, our cultural pendulum has now swung completely to the secular extreme. The current fad among radical feminists was mouthed by Barbara

Ehrenreich in a cover story for *TIME* magazine (March 1999).[8] They now want to be called *femaleists,* and they claim that women are more aggressive and promiscuous than men. The feminist movement that had requested opportunities equal to those enjoyed by men during Frances Willard's era became, in the 1990s, a movement that discounts the necessity of men's existence at all!

This is a philosophy that women in the coming century are supposed to celebrate? We need to take a giant leap back to look at the way God perceives history and gender. Christian women need the tools to publicly balance and defend what they profess theologically to combat the imbalances feminism has foisted on our culture.

The feminist "theology," when disassembled, is as incongruous as adding two and two and getting five. One need only examine the movement's response to the morality crisis in the Clinton White House to see that feminists are giving the answer five pretty consistently now, especially since the correct answer of four would damage their movement and their spokeswomen.

I was personally incredulous when I read an article on the Internet from the *Detroit Free Press* quoting Gloria Steinem and Anita Hill about why President Bill Clinton's sexual harassment scandal was not the same as Clarence Thomas allegedly saying "dirty words" to Anita Hill. To quote, "Hill also joined feminist leader Gloria Steinem in saying Sunday that Clinton's alleged advances to White House aide Kathleen Willey, while improper and crude if true, did not constitute sexual harassment."[9]

Their response didn't even proceed rationally if one were to dissect their argument, and yet the two women have made a good living touting this baloney, while the press gives them credibility. Come on, Anita and Gloria! Thinking women cannot possibly accept your rationale because it doesn't make sense! The answer is four, not five! I'm not buying it, nor is the majority of the female population out there! I want filet mignon from female spokeswomen, and you're giving me garbage!

One of the problems faced by today's feminists is that the subject matter they have foisted on our culture is, in reality, *not that deep*. Yet they want desperately for the culture to think that they have something profound to teach the dummies who "don't get it"! Feminists have managed to create curriculum called Women's Studies, which is often mandatory, in colleges, universities, and seminaries across the country, to validate their agenda. Prepare yourself for a look at some of these classes being offered by distinguished institutions, both public and private:

- Stanford University: Feminist Studies 240, "Lesbian Communities and Identities"
- University of Washington: Women's Studies 416, "Sexist Language and Education"; Women's Studies 456, "Feminism, Racism, and Anti-Racism"
- University of Michigan: English 315, "Crossing Erotic Boundaries: Representations of Lesbianism in Early Modern Western Europe"
- Rutgers University: American Studies 01:050:325, "Women on the Fringe: Perceptions of Women as Social and Sex-Role Deviants in American Civilization"
- University of Arizona: Women's Studies 430, "Lesbian/Bisexual Women's Theories/Lives/ Activisms."[10]

You get the picture. A course on the history of the feminist movement in the United States would be very interesting . . . as a single course or maybe even a couple of classes. But entire majors are built around this material now, and much of it focuses on lesbianism or women as victims.

Feminists will retain power and influence in politics and education only if they continue to create or invent new issues. The issues they are targeting usually pose women as the victims of white, oppressive males, and the culture as a hotbed of gender discrimination, sexual harassment, and misogyny. Quite frankly, it has become intensely tedious for me to look at the world through the eyes of these spokeswomen who portray all men as potential predators, rapists or abusers, or just plain mentally deficient.

The advertising world has completely bought into this feminist mindset, to the point that I often wonder if there are any men left in the industry at all! Don't any of them see what is obvious? I challenge you the reader to keep a pen handy while you watch television. Record how often the woman in the commercial is all-knowing, even when it comes to purchasing an automobile, and the male is a good-looking, dumb guy, just pleased as can be to have her lead him by the nose!

As an example, one Sunday I watched a televised NFL football game with my husband. Most of the commercials were for fast food or beer, but a few surprised me. Commercial advertisers would assume that the majority of folks watching this game would be men ... right? However, the feminist mindset has even broken into this "last bastion" of male dominance, because several ads depicted men as buffoons.

One portrayed an overweight man, who was obviously "the boss," trying to work a simple copy machine in the office. By the end of the commercial, he was covered with copy fluid and there were papers everywhere. His female assistant came to the rescue. Yes, the commercial was funny, but why wasn't this character a woman? The answer: It would be politically incorrect if a woman in a commercial was ever portrayed as an idiot.

Another commercial showed a man sitting on a sofa with a woman. He didn't want to watch the football game, but something "softer and more romantic" instead, while the woman wanted to watch the game. The ad industry portrayed the role reversal that feminists have coveted for the past twenty years ... the femaleist party line that women are more "manly" than men could ever hope to be! The woman has evolved into knowing more about the sport than the super-sensitive guy sitting by her on the sofa!

The caricature of men as nonessential bums made the headlines recently when *American Psychologist*, a journal of the American Psychological Association, printed an article written by Drs. Louise B. Silverstein and Carl F. Auerbach entitled "Deconstructing the Essential Father." "Having a father present in a family situation may be detrimental to the child and the mother," said the authors, given what they called the male tendency to consume "resources in terms of gambling, purchasing alcohol, cigarettes, or other nonessential commodities," which "increase[s] women's workload and stress."[11]

Women need to object loudly and clearly to this ridiculous portrait of men, husbands, and fathers. The authors of the above article are not the only ones in our culture who are making off-the-wall pronouncements! Read the following quotes from leading feminists and you will understand why the relationship between the sexes is in such turmoil:

> Under patriarchy, no woman is safe to live her life, or to love or to mother children. Under patriarchy, every woman is a victim, past, present and future. Under patriarchy, every woman's son is her potential betrayer and also the inevitable rapist or exploiter of another woman.[12]
>
> —Andrea Dworkin

> Patriarchy requires violence or the subliminal threat of violence in order to maintain itself. The most dangerous situation for a woman is not an unknown man in the street, or even the enemy in wartime, but a husband or lover in the isolation of their own home.[13]
>
> —Gloria Steinem

> All men are rapists and that's all they are.[14]
>
> —Marilyn French

The ultimate insult to men occurred at NOW's 1999 National Conference, where a "slam poet" named Alix Olson was given center stage. Lynn Vincent recounts in *World* magazine, "In her first poem, penned, she said, for her grandmother, Ms. Olson portrayed herself as a witch who swoops down on her broom to dismember men and make a stew of their vital body parts. In her second number, she fantasized about eradicating all males from her lineage (an interesting trick) and giving birth to herself aided only by women."[15] Vincent goes on to say that Olson received a standing ovation, the audience shouting for an encore. Is it puzzling why the majority of women today find it difficult to identify with NOW at the beginning of the new millennium?

One of the hazards of growing up in the foothills of Southern California was learning how to cope with natural predators indigenous to the terrain, one of which was the black widow spider. The black widow was easy to spot because she is particularly shiny black in color and has a red hourglass on her abdomen. The bites she gives are painful and poisonous, and one learned to be extremely wary around woodpiles, meter boxes, and the garage. I was afraid of this spider when I was growing up, especially when I learned the reason behind the name she was given: The black widow eats the male after mating. One of my friends, who is an ardent trivia buff, tells me that the black widow does this because the male is severely weakened after mating, and the female senses this and moves in for the kill.

How similar in technique the feminist movement has become to the black widow! Males are for disposal. First they are weakened by propaganda and legislation, and then they are devoured. Lesbianism is the logical extension of this philosophy because it is proof to the feminists that men truly are irrelevant.

The feminist movement discourages honest dialogue on issues, as many conservatives have learned somewhat painfully. If what you have to say is not politically correct, then it is fair game for ridicule. Make no mistake: There is a party line touted by powerful feminists that is as rigid as any that has existed in totalitarian governments! If that sentence sounds scary, it should! If you don't believe it, I place another challenge before you. Keep a pair of scissors by your side when you read the newspaper every day, and cut out the articles that have something to do with feminism or quotes from feminist spokeswomen.

I started doing this a number of years ago, and quite frankly, the file I accumulated was shocking. I wouldn't have believed the direction the movement was taking if I hadn't done this exercise over the years. In order to fight something as insidious as feminism, you need to know what the issues are. In the ensuing chapters, I hope to show you that:

- Feminism has destroyed standards of morality.
- Feminism has manipulated our language.
- Feminism has devastated same-sex friendships and become a movement dominated by the lesbian agenda.
- Feminism has resulted in a generation of men who disrespect and use women sexually.
- Feminism has distorted biblical teaching about roles and gender.
- Feminism has weakened the home and the family.
- Feminism has made women victims.

It doesn't take a genius with political savvy to realize that most feminist issues are liberal rather than conservative (for example, so-called "reproductive rights," lesbian rights, no-fault divorce, and so forth). It came as no surprise that the movement chose Bill and Hillary Clinton, the most powerful liberal couple in the country during his presidency (1993 through January 2001), as symbols of their philosophical program. Feminist spokeswomen protected the Clintons and that agenda at all costs, even when to do so actually resulted in hurting women who were true victims.

To illustrate, spokeswomen publicly defended the president when he was faced with sexual harassment complaints made by several women. Again, to quote from the *Detroit Free Press*, "Asked if a double standard exists in how women are looking at Clinton's actions, she [Anita Hill] said, 'We live in a political world, and the reality is there are larger issues other than just individual behavior.'"[16] Feminist journalist Nina Burleigh, former White House correspondent from *TIME*, was quoted as saying, in referring to President Clinton, "I'd be happy to give him [oral sex] just to thank him for keeping abortion legal."[17]

Betty Friedan was not far behind when she stated, "Even if he did what he's alleged to have done, what's the big deal? To have *our will* overthrown by a bunch of dirty, old white men trying to use sexual issues wrongly ... to impeach a president, this is really a disgrace to Washington, to the Congress, to the United States."[18] In other words, political power and the backing of the president on their feminist agenda was more important than justice to the women who had been wronged.

It is my belief that these feminist spokeswomen are fully aware of the outrageous hypocrisy of their remarks. Frances Willard and her cohorts in the WCTU fought for legislation that would protect women who had no civil rights whatsoever from being victims within society and within the construct of the family. They wanted women to have dignity within the marital bond, where abuse was not tolerated. But the spokeswomen of today's movement not only tolerated a president's disrespect and emotional abuse of women (*including* his wife and his daughter), but excused it because of his importance in promoting their agenda.

Does anyone feel pity toward Monica Lewinsky for allowing herself to be used and disrespected by one of the most powerful men in the world? Does anyone understand the complete humiliation foisted on his own daughter at an age when she is the most vulnerable? Does anyone think that his behavior added any dignity whatsoever to the office of the president or to the concerns of women? And yet we were supposed to celebrate him as a champion of women's rights!

At the height of the Lewinsky/Clinton scandal, Mrs. Clinton, in a televised interview, referred to the legal actions being pursued against her husband as a right-wing conspiracy, even going so far as to falsely mention a prominent Christian pastor as a perpetuator of this mean-spirited effort.[19] The press reported this across the country as fact. Personal accountability and truth were shoved aside, and the blame was tossed to political conservatives and the evangelical Christian community, which made no sense whatsoever.

Following the scandal, Mrs. Clinton was lauded as a heroine for her defense of her husband. Anyone with the temerity to say, "Hey, wait a minute! I disagree!" was criticized by feminists who used the tired cliché, "You're just threatened by strong women." Well, I am a strong woman, and I would challenge the heroine role given to our president's wife by her supporters!

Why would a feminist movement have ever been necessary historically if the party line since the 1990s has been to continue to celebrate as heroines women who allow themselves to be victimized repeatedly, particularly in a marital relationship? In this case, the "poor Hillary" story line, which was used by feminists to defend the First Lady, is a twisted logic that pictures all women whose husbands are sexual philanderers as "heroines" if they put up with, defend, and protect the behavior. This goes hand in hand with the feminist agenda, which in essence says that since all men are adulterers, it's just a cross Hillary and other women have to bear!

Well, *not all* men are adulterers. More importantly, adultery is public enemy #1 of a marriage, a fact recognized throughout Scripture. There is a time when a Christian woman confronts a sin that entirely disrespects her, says, "This has to stop" to her spouse, and lists consequences if he doesn't shape up! This type of abuse should never be tolerated or overlooked the first time it happens. To do so repeatedly is masochistic, and the Lord *never* designed women for the role of doormat.

The failure of the feminist movement in our culture today is that its leaders no longer understand the marketplace. They don't represent all women, only a marginalized few. But since they have influence with the power brokers who do define culture, they have the ability to reshape the way we think without the actual support of those they are supposedly representing … American women.

There is truth to the saying "Quit while you're ahead," but it's not human nature to do so. Feminists have to keep coming up with something new so their spokeswomen can earn big speakers' fees and claim to have credibility on nightly news programs. (Look at the yardage Anita Hill has gained because she once testified that Clarence Thomas supposedly talked dirty.) The early feminists have been lauded by historians for their accomplishments, as well they should have been. But the current batch of feminist spokeswomen leading the movement make their living complaining about their lot in life. This is exceedingly tiresome when you dissect their arguments and find thin air instead of substance.

To understand the dynamics of the feminist movement in the new millennium, one needs to fully comprehend its two main issues. These two battlefields are without question the areas of moral debate that separate their spokeswomen irreparably from evangelical Christians, and that define the cultural war we are in at this time in our nation's history. The two issues are reproductive rights, specifically abortion, and the promotion and legitimization of the lesbian lifestyle.

chapter 4

History Repeats Itself...Badly

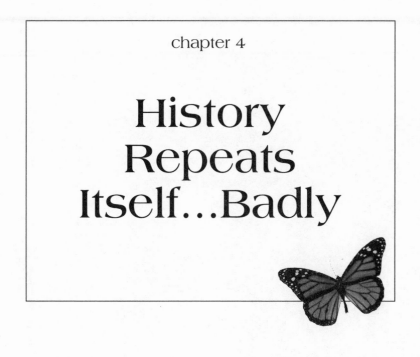

Susan was slow mentally, a child occupying a woman's body. I often wondered if she ever understood anything I said to her. Her usual response was an inappropriate burst of laughter, no matter what the subject matter. When she did talk, she came across as cocky and flippant. Susan was overweight, had severe acne, and no matter how carefully she groomed for my visits, she always had a bad hair day. She had grown up in an upper-middle-class home, but her parents never quite knew what to do with her. Her choice of friends was atrocious, and Tom, a member of a local motorcycle gang, became her constant companion. Between them, they created six babies, only one who lived. I was called in to be their Protective Services social worker when that tiny baby was hospitalized for starvation. While I had the case, Susan became pregnant a seventh time.

Elizabeth was another client. She resided in a dilapidated house in which it seemed that the entire roach population of Los Angeles also lived. I hated making house visits because Elizabeth never used sanitary napkins when she had her menstrual cycle; she sat on newspapers instead. Sometimes she would remember to discard them, and other times she wouldn't. The plumbing didn't work, so she cut a hole in the floor for the family to use as a toilet. The stench was unbearable. She had seven children, and her file in our office occupied a complete drawer. I became her Protective Services worker when one of her children tossed a match into the bed of another, causing third-degree burns on the boy's back. Hospital personnel were trying to decide if the child should return home or be placed in foster care. Elizabeth became pregnant with her eighth child while I had the case.

Janie was a beautiful young woman. Owners of the motel where she was living called to say that they heard her little girl screaming during the night. When I went to visit, Janie admitted that her new boyfriend didn't like her little girl because he was jealous of the attention that Janie gave to her. She told me she was breaking up with him because she was afraid he was becoming abusive, and that she would be moving to another city. During our entire conversation, she rocked her little girl and made cooing sounds in the child's ear.

I made a surprise home visit at her new address two days later, but she would not allow me in the door. I called the police, and after a forcible entry, Janie's little girl was found dead in the bathroom shower. In a fit of rage, the boyfriend had bashed her head against the wall, causing her death. The coroner later reported that the physical abuse on the child's body had been inflicted over a number of hours, and that she must have suffered terribly. At the trial, Janie told the court that she was pregnant with twins.

I had a Protective Services caseload for a number of years and handled hundreds of family situations as serious or more serious than those mentioned. I still have nightmares about cases that I have intentionally left out of this narrative because of the horror associated with them. These are the types of cases always cited by pro-choice advocates as the reason why we should never make abortion illegal again: Women like Susan, Elizabeth, and Janie shouldn't have children.

So . . . why am I now adamantly pro-life?

I wasn't always against abortion. When I graduated from UCLA in the late 1960s, I bought into the feminist, pro-choice argument just like every other woman I knew. The issue was in the news constantly, and *Roe v. Wade,* the Supreme Court decision legalizing abortion, was only a couple of years away from being handed down. My years as a caseworker occurred during the 1970s, after legalization of the procedure. Imagine the freedom I felt when

I could call Planned Parenthood for assistance in removing "the fetus" of a pregnant client who already had a history of inflicting abuse on her existing children. I felt like a savior, referring babies to be eliminated to save them from being abused later on. A baby didn't seem like a baby if you couldn't see it or if it was only "unwanted tissue" or a "fetus."

My perspective started to change only after I had a miserable pregnancy with my second child and almost miscarried a number of times. On one of those occasions, a neighbor drove me to the hospital, and my husband joined us there. I was bleeding profusely. I knew our baby was still alive because the fetal monitor indicated that there was a heartbeat. I didn't know that a drama was being enacted in the adjacent room where the attending physician was trying to talk my husband into aborting my baby. My husband was enraged that the medical personnel were trying to take a life rather than trying to save it.

Even though she was months from being full term, I *knew* our baby had a personality and was fully human. Yet I was still pro-choice, which meant intellectually agreeing with other pro-abortion advocates that pregnancies were only blobs of insensitive tissue! In hindsight, this wasn't even rational: I knew my unborn baby, whom I was struggling to keep alive within my womb, was a distinct person, yet I was in favor of killing other women's fully alive, human babies!

This is the basic inconsistency that defines the pro-life versus pro-death argument today. Feminists think it is completely rational to consider the pre-born child as human only if that child is *wanted*. Otherwise, the baby is just "a blob of tissue." This illogic plays out in bumper stickers: One of my friends saw a vehicle with these two slogans side by side: "Never Hurt a Child" and "Support a Woman's Right to Choose."

It wasn't until I learned how God perceived the unborn that I felt a deep repugnance for what I had been taught. I had bought the pro-abortion message completely, but had never gone to Scripture to see how the Lord viewed unborn children. The mainline church our family attended never gave the message about the sanctity of human life. I had no idea whatsoever that God views a child in the womb as precious. He knows who that child will become. He sees that child even though we cannot. I read Psalm 139 one day, and the words pierced my heart in such a physical way, it was as if I had been stabbed with a knife:

> For You formed my inward parts;
> You wove me in my mother's womb.
> I will give thanks to You, for I am fearfully and
>   wonderfully made;
> Wonderful are Your works,
> And my soul knows it very well.
> My frame was not hidden from You,
> When I was made in secret,
> And skillfully wrought in the depths of the earth.
> Your eyes have seen my unformed substance;
>   And in Your book were all written
> The days that were ordained for me,
> When as yet there was not one of them. (vv. 13-16)

I was never the same after I learned this psalm. Overnight, I became radically and unabashedly pro-life! I had it on the Highest Authority that a baby in the womb, no matter what stage of a pregnancy, is a human being with a soul and personality that our Lord acknowledges even before its presence becomes known to the mother. Abortion is a moral issue, not a political-rights issue that feminists define it to be for our culture.

This is a very important point because in our postmodern culture, expediency and personal happiness drive people and are among the reasons many women get abortions. The only way abortion ...

the brutal termination of pre-born babies ... can be sanctioned is if the issue is removed from the moral sphere and placed in the political sphere. Therefore, a Christian will hear the argument continuously, both within and outside of the church, that abortion should not be addressed from the pulpit. Feminists and their supporters have very successfully made it a political issue, when it is, in truth, a profoundly moral issue. Dr. Elizabeth Achtemeier expressed this so articulately in an essay she wrote for *Theology Matters*:

> For our God is the god who gives life instead of the death of the world. Right there, it seems to me, is the most radical contradiction to abortion—that God desires that all persons, whom he has created, live and not die. And surely the child in the womb is included in that number, for 'it is he that made us, and we are his' (Ps.100:3). He clothed us with skin and flesh and knit us together with bones and sinews (Job 10:11), until we emerged the wondrous, unique creatures that we are, each with our own DNA and fingerprints, our stature and our special voice. We clever human beings may fertilize human eggs in a petri dish or even clone ourselves, but God furnished the initial cells and the DNA, and apart from his creation of life, our science would be impossible. We come from God, and his purpose for all of us—born and unborn—is that we live.[1]

Abortion has become the hill on which feminists are willing to die. An entire generation of women has been so indoctrinated about abortion that to be a woman who is pro-life is to remove oneself to a so-called "right-wing fringe" referred to with ridicule by the media and entertainment industries. In many areas of the country, claiming to be pro-life is a "death sentence" for anyone running for public office. Feminists have carried out a campaign of indoctrination that is as methodical as the United States military preparing for Desert Storm. And they have emulated other movements in history that sought to destroy entire groups of human beings. For my purposes in this chapter, I will correlate the abortion movement in this country to what happened in the Nazi regime to "undesirables."

Feminists view pregnancy as a form of enslavement, and the baby as an intruder in the body. Feminist Shulamith Firestone writes, "Pregnancy is the temporary deformation of the body of the individual for the sake of the species."[2] The baby lacks humanity. It is an unnatural object that has invaded the body; never mind that it's usually as a result of the mother's sexual activity. What do you do with an unsightly mole? Get rid of it. What do you do with an unwanted pregnancy? Get rid of it. Abortion, the ultimate child abuse, is excusable if the baby is seen as an intruder. The baby is dehumanized, just as slaves were dehumanized prior to the Civil War, and just as Jews were dehumanized in Nazi Germany.

If a special-interest group—whether it be a political party, the policy makers in the South prior to the Civil War, or the leadership of Planned Parenthood—wants to effect change, it must first select its objective and then define the terms. If the objective was to eradicate the Jews in Germany, then the German people had to be convinced that the Jews were specifically responsible for the economic woes that plagued the country. Propaganda quickly changed this segment of the population to non-persons who could be annihilated without remorse.

Slave owners in the South would never have been permitted to enslave human beings, so they defined the personhood of blacks by allocating them to a sub-human category. The *Roe v. Wade* decision by our Supreme Court accomplished the same thing. Babies were not accorded the status of human beings with certain inalienable rights. The feminist dogma that babies were less human than the women who carried them prevailed.

My major in college was history, and my favorite subject matter was World War II. If you read about the Holocaust, you cannot help but feel horrified that the mass torture and murder of millions of Jews was carried out by German soldiers who had been "ordinary people" at one point in their lives. How could "normal" people work at the death camps and not rebel against what they saw and were asked to do every day?

The same question could be asked of "ordinary" people in our country before the Civil War and prior to the Civil Rights movement. They were blind to the suffering of blacks; it didn't matter because it was a way of life. The same could be said of the sweat shops that existed prior to legislation outlawing child labor. How could people be blind to what was happening to children, especially when they were severely maimed by equipment in these hell-holes?

What about today? Millions of babies have been cruelly murdered, and we turn our backs on it. The economy is of more interest than mass murder. After all, it's done so quietly and so cleanly. Doctors in sterile uniforms are present, and the clinics are professional in every way! It couldn't be as bad as pro-lifers say it is!

Carol Everett, author of *The Scarlet Lady*, ran an abortion clinic before becoming a Christian. She oversaw or participated in 35,001 abortions at the facility. She writes, "I spent six years of my life with abortionists, not physicians. They did not preserve life. They destroyed it—sometimes the mother, every time the baby. ...When we finished the violent act of killing the baby, we took it to the central supply room, reassembled and counted the parts, put them down the commercial, heavy-duty garbage disposal and turned it on. We listened as the blades shredded the head, body, arms, legs, hands, and feet."[3]

I don't think we as a country can arrogantly say that the Holocaust could never happen here. It's happening every day in abortion clinics in every city and state, except we use a garbage disposal instead of a crematorium.

Christian author and commentator Ravi Zacharias writes, "Imagine yourself caught in the middle of a conversation at a professors' luncheon discussing the issue of child abuse. Imagine your reaction should you find that there were both protagonists and antagonists—some in favor of it, while others condemn it. It would stagger the imagination to think that some would defend the victimization of a child. Common sense alone dictates the rationale behind the protection and care of the most innocent and vulnerable of our society."[4]

Yet in our universities today, as well as on nightly news programs, the legacy of the feminist love affair with abortion is that there will inevitably be a debate pitting someone who is pro-life against someone who is pro-choice. Whereas most people would be appalled at anyone who took a pro-child-abuse role in a debate, they accept without question a debate regarding child abuse in the womb. It has become an abstract issue rather than a life-and-death issue involving a child.

A tactic that the feminist movement has used very effectively today to confuse women is the manipulation of language. Dr. Charles Carroll, one of my most treasured friends, was an official observer at the Nuremberg Trials (1945-1949), where German physicians were tried for crimes against humanity following World War II. He states that the way in which our language today is manipulated to be politically correct is the same tactic employed by the Nazi regime in the late 1930s to convince the German people of the inhumanity of the Jews, which then could justify their slaughter. Correlate this with the way the feminists have justified their pro-choice position by a clever use of words. Abortion is the "removal of unwanted tissue" instead of the intentional killing of a growing child. The term *fetus* is substituted for *baby* to dehumanize the infant. To quote Father Carroll, an Episcopal clergyman, in an interview published in *Focus on the Family Citizen,*

A woman doesn't carry an unborn child today; she carries a "fetus." A girl who in my time was promiscuous is today "sexually active." We have robbed everything of morality, and we have denied the child in the womb. As surely as we robbed the slave of his personhood and the Jew of his personhood, at the Nuremberg Trials, we did it to the unborn child. One of the interesting things about the Nazi revolution is that Germany was in a moral vacuum. And moral vacuums, like natural vacuums, cry to be filled. You only have to pick up a few books and read about life in Berlin during the 1920s. One of the saddest stories I read was of a family that was hard-pressed to survive, so they invited their friends to cocktails or tea and offered their daughters in the bedroom at a certain fee. And look at what is going on in this country: A woman driving her children into a lake; a woman going into the ladies room, having a child, throwing it in a dumpster and going back to the prom; partial-birth abortions.[5]

How has abortion become such an accepted everyday practice that it is not an issue for so many women? Why is it so important for women to have "control over their bodies" so that they have the freedom to pursue their lifestyle, education, and career plans without the impediment of pregnancy? During Frances Willard's lifetime (1838-1898), there was at least moral consensus in the way the majority of women approached life. Children were an accepted part of that life. The law of the land, similar in many ways to a compass, mirrored the Christian values that most women lived by.

But a compass isn't any good if it doesn't point true north or magnetic north. The law cannot be a compass for society if it flexes with whatever is politically correct. We kid ourselves if we still believe that we have a system of laws based on an absolute moral code that everybody understands. What we have today is itself a religion ... a religion of hostility to God and the moral code He established in Scripture ... and it has been codified by legislators and the judiciary.

In Nazi Germany, the law and morality became separate entities. Charles Carroll wrote in the *United States Air Force Journal of Legal Studies*: "Consider (that) the Nuremberg Laws, which were hastily drafted at 2:30 A.M. in the morning of September 15, 1935, on a requisitioned menu card at the villa of Wilhelm Frick, Nazi Minister of the Interior, robbed the German Jews of their citizenship, their personhood, and, in all too many instances, their lives."[6] The expropriation, concentration, deportation, and extermination of Jews was all part of a *legal* process in Germany.

Hitler established law based on his personal ethics and agenda. With the exception of a few martyrs, such as Dietrich Bonhoeffer, *the mainline Church toed the Nazi party line.* Law apart from a moral code *always* results in victims. When *Roe v. Wade* became the law of our land, law again became separated from morality. Except for a few notable Christian spokesmen, *the mainline Church toed the feminist pro-abortion line.* In Germany, the victims were the Jews. In the United States, the victims are the babies.

In 1798, President John Adams stated in a speech to the military, "We have no government armed with power capable of contending with human passions unbridled by morality and religion. Avarice, ambition, revenge, or gallantry would break the strongest cords of our Constitution as a whale goes through a net. Our Constitution was made only for a moral and religious people. It is wholly inadequate to the government of any other."[7]

Consider that our United States Supreme Court has granted "legal" personhood to corporations in the *Dartmouth College Case* and in *The County of Santa Clara v. The Southern Pacific Railroad Company* but denied it to a man in the case involving Dred Scott and, of course, in *Roe v. Wade.* In other words, inanimate objects, specifically corporations, were given the same rights enjoyed by humans, such as the right to sue or to own property, but slaves and the unborn were denied human rights. In *Roe v. Wade*, the Court insisted that the "Constitution did not define 'person' in so many words. ... None [of three references to person in the Fourteenth Amendment] adds with any assurance that it has any pre-natal application."[8] Does this make any sense whatsoever? Corporations are human, but humans are not? Morality based on biblical text that human beings are created in the image of their Divine Creator has been separated from law at the highest level in our land.

The tragedy that occurred when *Roe v. Wade* became law was that mainline denominations took an abrupt departure from their historical views of theology and separated "the soul" from the physical body in the unborn. In other words, they completely bought into the feminist viewpoint that the unborn child was only a mass of tissue, incapable of feeling, incapable of having any human attributes that would make it a person. The mainline denominations went as far as to form organizations such as the Religious Coalition for Reproductive Rights, which put them directly in league with organizations such as Planned Parenthood and NARAL (National Abortion Rights and Action League) by advocating the killing of unborn children.

Thomas F. Torrance, a contemporary of Charles Carroll, and an eminent theologian in his own right, stated in a speech before the Scottish Order of Christian Unity in Edinburgh, "The human embryo is *fully human being, personal being* in the sight and love of his or her Creator, and must be recognized, accepted, and cherished as such, not only by his or her mother and father, but by science and medicine."[9] Torrance stated that the human life of Jesus Christ began at the moment of His conception in the womb of Mary, His mother, and further stated that that was precisely the basis for the early Church to reject abortion and infanticide.[10]

Feminists make a big deal out of the statement, "Well, we really don't know when life begins. It is arguable that it begins at conception." In an excellent essay in *The Post-Abortion Review*, edited by Dr.

David Reardon, there appears this statement: "With an honesty often missing from the current abortion debate, the pro-choice editors of *California Medicine* affirm that 'everyone really knows' that human life begins at conception. *Everyone* knows it. Every denial is simply 'semantic gymnastics' offered by 'socially impeccable auspices' to ease our way."[11]

In 1972 Senator James L. Buckley gave a speech at St. Frances College in which he stated, "Those who propose abortion today will propose infanticide and euthanasia tomorrow."[12] Tragically, that is precisely what has occurred in our country with the partial-birth abortion procedure. I know that many don't understand what partial-birth abortion is, and when the procedure is described, they simply don't believe that such a process is legal in the United States of America. However, this procedure *is* legal and performed routinely. It is the inhumane killing of viable babies in the third trimester of life—many times *full term*—*without* the use of anesthesia, immediately prior to delivery, by an abortionist. The physician turns the baby and delivers all but the head, thrusts scissors into the base of the skull, inserts a suction catheter to remove the brain, and then completes the delivery of the now dead infant.

One would hope ... would think ... that no rational, feeling human being would support such a procedure, and yet feminists state that it is a necessity if we are truly going to have reproductive freedom. Again, politicians have dealt with it as if it is a political issue, rather than a moral issue with the lives of babies in the balance. What would they think if they were in an abortion clinic observing this procedure firsthand? On three occasions during his term in office, President William Clinton vetoed legislation that would have made this procedure illegal.

The National Abortion Federation claims that a mere one-half of 1 percent of all abortions are performed after 20 weeks, which translates into 20 late-term abortions a day in America. One clinic in New Jersey admitted performing 15,000 per year!

(Approximately 1.4 million abortions [close to 3800 per day] are performed in the United States per year, according to statistics reported in *USA Today,* August 14, 1996, attributed to the Alan Guttmacher Institute.[13] Current estimates of pro-life organizations put that number higher, at approximately 4400 per day.) This is infanticide pure and simple. These are *viable* babies, but to listen to the feminists like Congresswoman Barbara Boxer defend the procedure, they could be just clumps of cow manure.

Now let's reflect back on how the Nazis justified medical experiments on unanesthetized prisoners in concentration camps: It became common to refer to these subjects as "human material," according to Charles Carroll. The rationale used by the German physicians was that these people were going to die anyway, so why not use them as experimental objects in order to develop treatments that would benefit everyone? Are babies now "human material" for feminists who consider full-term infants appropriate subjects for medical annihilation and experimentation? What if the "human material" was a woman who was having a cancerous tumor purposefully inserted in a non-cancerous breast, without anesthesia, for the sake of medical experimentation? Would feminists scream about that? You bet they would! But they never scream for an innocent baby! *And what about the rest of our culture? The silence is deafening.*

To add the ultimate insult to these aborted babies, their body parts are being marketed and sold, thanks to legislation signed by President Clinton in 1993.[14] The National Institutes of Health Revitalization Act in effect lifted the ban on federally funded research involving fetal tissue. Gene Rudd, an obstetrician and member of the Christian Medical and Dental Society's Bioethics Commission, is quoted in *World* magazine: "When we fail to see life as sacred and ordained by God as unique, this is the reasonable conclusion ... taking whatever's available to gratify our own self-interests and taking the weakest of the species first ... like jackals. This is the inevitable slide down the slippery slope."[15]

Abortion is big business and very profitable. Now we have an added dimension for the "doctors" who make a livelihood in this way: There is money to be made in selling baby body parts. Again, *World* magazine reported the results of an investigation behind the scenes in the abortion industry: "The probe unearthed grim, hard-copy evidence of the cross-country flow of baby body parts, including detailed dissection orders, a brochure touting 'the freshest tissue available,' and price lists for whole babies and parts. One 1999 price list from a company called Opening Lines reads like a cannibal's wish list: Skin $100. Limbs (at least 2) $150. Spinal cord $325. Brain $999 (30% discount if significantly fragmented)."[16]

The newest battleground is the attack at the other end of the life cycle, the euthanasia movement. Although euthanasia is not identified as part of the feminist agenda, it is directly related to their love affair with abortion. If life is disposable at one end of the spectrum, then why not at the other? And if it's legal to kill an innocent baby, then why not senior citizens and the disabled? After all, they are a drain on our nation's resources, aren't they? This segment of our population is currently the focal point of the pro-death forces.

Let's not manipulate language here! Feminists and supporters of euthanasia have intentionally called this "mercy death" instead of using such harsh words as "murder." Again, they have the Nazis to thank for doing some of the homework for them. According to Father Charles Carroll, Hitler's experts went through several word definitions in an attempt to soften the meaning of euthanasia, including such terms as "redemptive death" and "help to die" before settling on the term "mercy death."

Father Carroll, in a speech before an audience of retired military officers shortly before the 50th anniversary remembrance of the Holocaust, related the history of euthanasia for the German people prior to World War II. The elderly and mentally ill were placed in facilities where they would spend their final days.

Medication was given to ease their suffering, but when this became too expensive, the decision was made to withhold food and water instead. When the cries of the starving patients became too much for the caretaker staff to endure, then the idea of "gassing" the patients was born. And anyone can guess what this transitioned to ... the gas chambers where millions of Jews were exterminated.

I can remember the slow deaths of both of my grandfathers, yet these men added a special dimension to my life, even as they suffered. Some of the most poignant and meaningful conversations we ever had were when they were at death's door. At any point in time, a person in the midst of depression or desperation can say that he no longer wants to live, but the Lord has always been the One who determines the number of our days. Christians have a tough time understanding why Corrie ten Boom, who survived a Nazi concentration camp and carried the gospel to the far corners of the globe, had to be in a coma for so long before she died. We won't know answers to questions like these until we see the Father face to face. But human beings have not been given the authority by God to kill other human beings except in very limited circumstances, and abortion and euthanasia aren't among them.

I know that numerous women reading this book have had abortions. Many of the Christian women I work with at Focus on the Family have had abortions. In many ways, the woman who has had an abortion is as much a victim as the baby she lost. It is "beyond pain" to deal with the grief of the past, and yet we have a phenomenal Savior who tells us in the Bible that our sins are completely forgiven because of what He accomplished when He died for us on a tree. Because of this, I *know* that I am forgiven for the sins I perpetuated by touting abortion to my social services clients who were pregnant. Carol Everett knows that she is forgiven for once running an abortion clinic. And I know that any woman reading this who has had an abortion is also forgiven.

We may always feel the guilt associated with our mistakes, but Jesus has cleansed us of those mistakes. Again ... the Bible says that they are *forgotten:*

> For as high as the heavens are above the earth,
> So great is His lovingkindness toward those who fear
>   Him.
> As far as the east is from the west,
> So far has He removed our transgressions from us.
> Just as a father has compassion on his children,
> So the Lord has compassion on those who fear Him.
> (Psalm 103, vv. 11-13)

Because of what we have endured, and because of the forgiveness we have received, we can become powerful spokeswomen for the truth about abortion and what it does to the women who have them. We can become advocates for the unborn by actively demonstrating on their behalf. Our culture has criticized pro-life demonstrators who have picketed abortion clinics, even though we all know what is going on behind those doors. The media is quick to point out the violence perpetuated by a few against abortionists, yet the vast majority of Christians would condemn that as well. (You cannot be pro-life and pro-death at the same time.)

If the babies being crushed were two years old instead of infants in the womb, wouldn't everybody be outside demonstrating? Is it a matter of age? Again, the feminist love affair with abortion is so entrenched in our culture that opponents are ridiculed for doing precisely what the Lord would commend ... making a visible stand for the "least of these."

It is ironic that the peaceful prohibition movement sit-in that occurred in 1873 in Hillsboro, Ohio, could easily describe the non-violent Christian demonstrations in which women participate today in front of abortion clinics. Yet today's protests are deemed illegal and subject to prosecution under RICO (Racketeer Influenced and Corrupt Organizations Act) legislation. Our heritage is one of effective non-violent protest when women were without rights, but now that we have civil rights, protest is an option for women only if it is politically correct! Abortion is a women's issue, yet protest has been stifled by ... you guessed it ... women!

One other way that women can become involved is by volunteering at their local crisis pregnancy centers. So many case studies of women who have had abortions are tragic; they felt they had no choices, even when they didn't want to abort the child growing inside them. They are either living with the truth of the event or they are still running from it. Redemption from sin can be worked out in such a beautiful way when our mistakes are turned around to help others who find themselves in the same "hopeless" predicament. These centers are making a tremendous impact across the country, and babies are celebrating birthdays in loving homes as a result.

One reason thinking women, whether Christian or non-Christian, are becoming disillusioned with the rhetoric of prominent feminists regarding abortion is that there are so many inconsistencies in their arguments when it comes to "sexual freedom":

- If feminists want women to be perceived as masters of their own destiny, then why are irresponsibility and lack of self-control the reasons behind most elective abortions? It has become a method of birth control.
- If feminists consider men disposable (as well as babies), then why are men *not* disposable if a woman elects to keep her baby and requires support?
- Women glorify their new sense of sexual freedom, but when they get pregnant, they criticize men for being unwilling to make a "commitment."

- Why do feminists say that kids should say no to drugs but not to sex? Both activities damage the body. Many incurable venereal diseases are now at epidemic proportions among women.
- Why do feminists, who support the dignity and status of women, defend "sex selection" abortion, which more often kills female babies?

It is obligatory for the Christian community to be the instrument to challenge feminists about their rigidity on the issue of abortion because they have made reproductive rights their battle cry through the years. Recent data is hopeful; our culture appears to be slowly changing its mind about the "religious dogma" of the left that abortion is the *right* of every female. A recent *Associated Press* article authored by Richard N. Ostling reports that the Center for Gender Equality, a liberal women's think tank run by Faye Wattleton (the former president of Planned Parenthood), took a poll of 1000 American women. A full 53 percent responded that abortion should be allowed only in cases of rape, incest, or to save the mother's life. This figure is up from 45 percent recorded in 1996. Women also indicated that religion was "very important" in their lives (75 percent).[17] There is still a long way to go, especially when partial-birth abortion remains legal in this country.

God created human beings to be stewards of His creation. This is clear in Scripture in the first chapter of Genesis when God created man and gave him dominion over all the living creatures and vegetation. We can also reference the parable of the talents in Matthew 25 where the Lord commends two men who invested wisely, but disdains the unprofitable servant. We are caretakers of the Lord's creation, especially when it comes to "the least of these." An abortionist chooses to be God when he assumes the role of taking an innocent baby's life. James 4:12 reads, "There is one Lawgiver, who is able to save and to destroy" (NKJV). Who knows what a certain unborn baby will become? *Only God.*

I have come to realize most profoundly the illogic in the argument that if abortion were not an option for pregnant women, our society would be filled with abused and unwanted children. The feminists have had their way with making abortion the solution for abuse, yet anyone who pays attention knows that child abuse statistics are worse than ever. Newspapers make no secret of this.[18] It is glaringly obvious that the legalization of abortion *did not* eradicate the abuse of children in our culture.

We may have the opinion certain women should never be parents, but that does not make the case that the child created by one of these women isn't valuable. Maybe the rationale should be that we kill the mother instead of the baby! Okay, that is an outrageous statement. But, in that context, think about the lack of logic in killing an innocent child because of the lifestyle of the mother! Aren't feminists selling *all* women short, even those who have had a history with Protective Services, like the three women I mentioned at the beginning of this chapter? Aren't they saying that it is impossible for people to change?

In effect, this reasoning reduces all women who choose to carry a baby rather than abort to the category of future child abusers: "*If we don't kill them now, their moms may abuse them in the future.*" Research is now being reported that links abortion to lower crime rates in our country.[19] If abortion is lowering the crime rate, perhaps we should continue this line of illogic and just kill everyone we think will commit a crime so we can eradicate crime forever.

Feminists imply that God's creation is beyond His redemption; they believe that God can't reach you if you are poor, or in a problem pregnancy, or have a history of child abuse. Look at what the Lord did for Joseph. The man was in a dungeon for years after his brothers sold him into slavery, but the Lord redeemed him from the pit. Years later, Joseph was able to say to his brothers, "But as for you, you meant evil against me; but God meant it for good" (Genesis 50:20, NKJ). Our Lord can *always* work for the good of a woman suffering from an unplanned and difficult pregnancy: "And we know that God causes all things to work together for good to those who love God, to those who are called according to His purpose" (Romans 8:28).

When I was a Protective Services caseworker, I often became discouraged, but I never gave up on any of my clients. I saw such potential in each of them. The sweetness of the Christian faith is seeing the Lord accomplish miracles in impossible situations. Dr. Elizabeth Achtemeier expresses it beautifully:

> The Christian faith calls us, therefore, to that life-giving surrender to our Father, in which we trust his purpose in making us and our unborn children in the first place, and then further rely on him to guide and provide for us and our child, no matter what our circumstances. Yes, children interrupt our lifestyle and comfort; they require our money; some of them may seem to have the most dismal futures; and goodness knows, we never can control them, much less ourselves, to our satisfaction. But God has willed our children in his creative purpose and we continue to trust him with our lives and theirs. That trust is the way of life and not the way of death. And it is radically different from the ways of the world.[20]

The feminists use abortion as the solution for incredible social problems, including child abuse, unwanted pregnancies, and dysfunctional parenting ... specifically those family situations I mentioned at the beginning of this chapter. But if the solution is death, then there is no need for any of the helping professions. Why do we need social workers and mental health workers, whose calling is the hope of effecting significant change in the lives of hurting adults and their children? And further, why would we need the church or the pastorate if we didn't believe that change is possible? Christians serve a God who is still in the business of doing miracles in the lives of everyday people like you and me.

Can we really trust that God cares about each life, regardless of the circumstances to which he or she is born? Consider Teri: She and her many siblings were the illegitimate children of two drug addicts. Her father was a notorious drug dealer in Southern California. Because she was born addicted to amphetamines, she was removed from her mother's custody shortly after birth and placed in an emergency shelter home. Wouldn't this terribly ill little girl have been better off if she had never been born? Feminists would say so!

But the Lord had a plan for this little girl, and she wasn't placed in just any emergency care facility: Her foster parents were Christians. This couple eventually adopted Teri, and she now has a new name and a new family. Her papa is a vice president at Focus on the Family, and he calls her "his princess." The addicted, underweight little girl who came into the world unloved is now "royalty," and she loves the Lord with all her heart. She *knows* she was created in the image of God! *He* doesn't make mistakes.

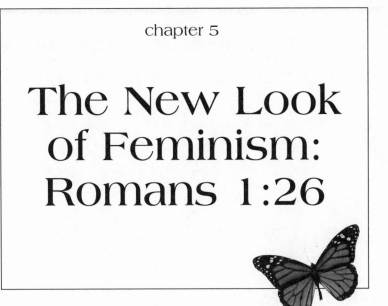

chapter 5

The New Look of Feminism: Romans 1:26

Christians, for the most part, have floundered when dealing with the issue of homosexuality. They rarely get help from the pulpit, which has struggled historically in dealing with the subject of sexuality and sexual sin as Sunday morning sermon material. I am among the minority of Americans that is in church regularly on Sunday mornings. I can recall only one sermon over the years that dealt with pornography. Amidst the immorality of our culture, sexual perversion and what the church would call sexual sin have expanded by leaps and bounds. Porn sites and chat rooms are readily available on the Internet. Society's behavioral patterns reflect the truth: Adultery and premarital sex are no longer the taboos of yesteryear.

I received a telephone call from a former employee late one Friday evening. She was asking for a job reference, which startled me. I knew she had four children under ten years of age and was a stay-at-home mom. This young mother was struggling to find employment so she could feed her children. She had married an extremely talented young man who excelled at writing music. I was completely shocked to learn that her husband had deserted the family several months earlier because of his addiction to pornography on the Internet. He had begun to act out his sexual fantasies with a number of women. Pornography had become more important to him than his wife and family.

There are tragic results when a person has a sexual addiction. Pornographers will fight until their last breath for their First Amendment rights to free expression despite the consequences that befall the innocent. Cigarette manufacturers have been punished for selling a substance that is damaging to health, yet pornography is allowed to flourish, and four little children who lost their dad will never get their justice. Nor will the young teens whose lives have been irrevocably changed as they struggle with an incurable venereal disease because they bought into the sexual freedom message that the entertainment industry has promoted at such enormous profit.

The Bible defines homosexuality as sexual sin. But Christians are as confused as the rest of our culture regarding how to deal with this issue. One reason is because homosexuality has hit so close to home for many of us. We may have family members whom we deeply care for who are homosexual, as well as neighbors, or perhaps a close friend at work. We struggle with the head knowledge that the two women watering their garden next door are condemned in Scripture for their behavior, yet our hearts care about them so much.

There is a huge gap in public conduct between most of the homosexual people we know and the lesbian activists in the headlines and in the parades who are so offensive. Lesbians come in so many shapes and forms ... they cannot be stereotyped. They may include the homecoming queen who appears as feminine as a cover girl, or the campus tomboy who excels in athletics. They can be raised in Christian homes or in homes where the Lord's name is only a swear word.

Another reason Christians struggle is because homosexual activists have been so successful in convincing our culture that anyone who considers homosexuality as a sin is "intolerant," or worse, a hate monger. Some Christians reinforce this by acting a little scary around gays: They can be eloquent in pointing out why homosexual behavior is defined as sexual sin, but they have a tough time communicating the message of the love of Christ that will free them from that sin. Sexual sin that takes place between unmarried heterosexual lovers doesn't get quite the same hell-and-damnation treatment as homosexual sin, and yet Scripture is clear that both are offenses in the eyes of a holy God (1 Corinthians 6:9-10).

One of our Focus on the Family staff members was once deeply involved in the homosexual lifestyle. In fact, Amy was the press secretary for the National Organization for Women, had a lesbian lover, and was very much involved in gay politics. She has an incredible testimony about her conversion to Christianity, but she says, "Part of my confusion stemmed from the fact that I couldn't reconcile my heart's yearning with the hostile behavior I encountered in some Christians. Rarely did I see anyone reflecting the heart or nature of God pursuing me."[1]

One of Amy's friends, who was also at one time a participant in the gay lifestyle, dropped into my office to chat recently. He became a Christian after a loving couple ministered to him personally at a very low point in his life when he was ill. Their Christ-like behavior eventually led to his incredible conversion. He said, "Everyone is into labels … 'lesbian,' 'gay,' 'right wing,' 'left wing.' We need to look at people as individuals. Many homosexuals were once victims as children. They have pain and baggage. We need to minister to the person and not the label and tell him or her about the transforming power of Christ." Great advice! And it is possible to do so *without* editing Scripture!

Although it may be intimidating, educated Christian women need to be able to address this pertinent social issue as well as articulately explain the incredible plan and design of the Creator for males and females, not only to their peers in the workplace, but to their sons and daughters, neighbors and friends. The feminist agenda embraces lesbianism to such an extent that this behavior now defines the movement. Feminist leadership is so far out in left field that most women in this country aren't listening anymore. But the spokeswomen do have the ear of the entertainment industry, the media, universities, and certain politicians, who have the power to redefine the way our culture views same-sex unions. Evangelical

Christians can no longer be silent on this issue and hope that it goes away because that "ain't gonna happen."

Not all lesbians believe as their activist spokeswomen do, and we need to understand that point clearly. However, there is a thread that binds feminist and lesbian activists that needs to be defined. Both groups see themselves as a minority oppressed by a larger cause, whether that cause be defined as "the Church," oppressive white men, or "the system." If you are a woman who is sexually confused or who had an abusive childhood at the hands of your father or another male, you ache for acceptance ... for an identity. Feminism is the established vehicle through which you can express your frustration and feel safe.

Lesbian activists grabbed onto the feminist freight train with gusto. It has been a very convenient coupling. Both groups are anti-Christian; the servanthood message of the gospel is seen as oppression. Both groups see parenting, raising a child, as a function that can occur without a male counterpart. Both groups oppose leadership by men and desire autonomy from men. Both groups feel that gender roles are culturally constructed, and that there is no difference between men and women except the artificial roles assigned them at birth by our culture.

Why do I contend that NOW has become the mouthpiece for the lesbian culture? Let us look at two conferences: NOW's 1999 National Conference in Beverly Hills, California, which I briefly referred to in the third chapter, and the April 1999 Lesbian Rights Summit sponsored by NOW in Washington, D.C.

A meager 800 attendees showed up at the Beverly Hills conference. Lynn Vincent, a writer for *World* magazine, was in attendance, and wrote, "At the Beverly Hilton, female couples held hands in the ballroom and strolled arm-in-arm through corridors, wearing rainbow buttons with the slogan, 'Ask and I'll tell.' More than half the contents of the purple vinyl conference packet issued to each attendee was devoted to gays and lesbians; two-thirds of the material displayed on the only information table inside the International Ballroom was lesbian-oriented. And at least half the entertainers on tap were lesbians."[2]

At the Washington, D.C., conference, a primary spokeswoman was Urvashi Vaid, the director of the Policy Institute of the National Gay and Lesbian Task Force. Her remarks were especially revealing: "Lesbian activists ... need to forego the 'politics of inclusion'— which have brought us a long way—and become louder and more confrontational.... The politics of inclusion are easy. What's harder is how to build the kind of government we want. . . . Homophobia ... does not occur in a vacuum. It's institutionalized in government, law, *churches*, the *family*, and other institutions."[3] I intentionally emphasized the words *churches* and *family* because by singling out these two institutions, Vaid and her lesbian colleagues have declared war on Christianity.

Dr. James Dobson is often the target of criticism by feminists because he has carried the banner for the traditional family for so long. But many other prominent Christian spokesmen have also been critical of the feminist/lesbian movement and its goal to dismantle this basic human institution ordained by God. In a September 1999 speech in Denver, Colorado, Kay Arthur stated that our country will be destroyed if the family is destroyed, and added, "There is nothing feminine about the feminist movement." She received a resounding ovation from the hundreds of women in attendance.

Janet Parshall has offered similar sentiments on her nationally syndicated radio broadcast *Janet Parshall's America!*. In a book co-authored with her husband, Craig, entitled *Tough Faith*, they make reference to the false doctrines of homosexual and feminist activists who have attempted to redefine and edit the Scripture:

> Let us have the courage to admit that the rise of these heretical forms of belief are not someone else's responsibility.

They are *our* responsibility. Those who propagate these false messages, and those who believe them, are creating for themselves not just false systems of belief, but dangerous mirages that take thirsty people and lead them into a desert. Damage is being done to people, and lives are being destroyed. We must be the water carriers with the living water of Jesus Christ.[4]

The creation of the family was directed by an almighty, sovereign God, and no women's movement, no matter how loud and angry, can change that fact. The message of the gospel is one of incredible *love*, but perfectly balanced by *justice*. How does a Christian articulate that to a woman who is caught up in lesbianism, or who has never grasped the concept of a loving heavenly Father because her biological father was dysfunctional? Let's go back to Christianity 101!

The Trinity was a love story before God created mankind; God the Father, Jesus Christ the Son, and the Holy Spirit, each loving and serving one another in a way that our finite minds will never completely understand. But the design was so perfect that God the Father created a similar pattern when He made man and woman, a triangle, so to speak, with God at the head, and Adam and Eve at each angle. In Genesis 2:20 we are told that in all the species the Lord had created, there was not a suitable helper for Adam, the first human being He created. At this point in time, God could have made another Adam, or even given a larger role to "man's best friend" and designated Rin Tin Tin or Air Bud for the position. But He didn't do that: He created woman *from* man … "bone of my bones, And flesh of my flesh" (v. 23).

In the Fall, recorded in Genesis 3, we are told that the woman ate the fruit of the tree that had been expressly designated as off-limits by God the Father, and that she shared that fruit with Adam. God banished Adam and Eve from the Garden of Eden, and they and their heirs were condemned to lives of harsh back-breaking labor and pain in childbirth, followed eventually by physical death. But God the Father, because of His great love for mankind, had a plan for redemption of the human race.

After the Fall, Eve was subordinated to Adam (Genesis 3:16). This is the foundation of the patriarchal family unit. But God uses the authority structure for the family that He designed in Genesis in a marvelous way: He redeems woman's mistake in the Fall by allowing Mary to be the conduit through which a "new Adam" is born ... Jesus Christ, without sin and through whom we have eternal life! All of us now have the invitation to live forever with God because, through Jesus Christ, we become children of God. The spiritual DNA that believers possess is that of children of God. We are not "employees" in the Garden of Eden ... we are *children* of our Creator God.

When a man and woman unite in marriage, they have achieved the greatest measure of human intimacy possible here on earth. Yet we cannot comprehend the intimacy that we will have with our God when we go to heaven. That is precisely why God says repeatedly in Scripture that homosexuality is an offense to Him: It denies the great "love story" that He designed. He made male and female as the perfect complement to each other. Ex-gays will tell you that promiscuity is rampant in the homosexual community, but the case could be made that the same holds true for the heterosexual singles community. This is because any relationship outside of God's design will not satisfy the human beings He created.

Feminists have equated sex with power and freedom, and the promiscuity of females for the past two decades, the tacit approval to "sleep around," has been the result. The lesbian movement takes this thought line a step further and says that to be truly a feminist, one must be lesbian. Men are simply not necessary. God's perfect plan is absolutely denied.

Romans 1:26-27 could have been written in the 1990s: "For this reason God gave them over to degrading passions; for their women exchanged the natural function for that which is unnatural, and in the same way also the men abandoned the natural function of the woman and burned in their desire toward one another, men with men committing indecent acts and receiving in their own persons the due penalty of their error." And the condemnation expressed in Romans 1:32 also applies for many of today's church denominations as well: "Although they know the ordinance of God, that those who practice such things are worthy of death, they not only do the same, but also give hearty approval to those who practice them."

Hank Hanegraaff writes in his book *The Face That Demonstrates the Farce of Evolution* that evolutionists as far back as Sir Julian Huxley have tried to argue God out of existence because *God interferes with the sexual mores of a culture.*[5] Feminists have been incredibly successful in this regard, but what are the results? Single moms, absent fathers, rampant venereal disease, AIDS, pornography, abortion. Nice job, ladies!

Hanegraaff states the obvious: "Attempting to rationalize God out of existence in order to do away with His laws of morality is as absurd as voting to repeal the law of gravity because people have fallen off of buildings, bridges, or boats. Even a unanimous vote could not change the deadly consequences for someone who later attempts to jump off of a ten-story building. We cannot violate God's physical or moral laws without suffering disillusionment, destruction, and even death."[6]

As I indicated in chapter three of this book, feminists want to be called *femaleists* now because they think of themselves as being more aggressive and more promiscuous than men. Again, lesbians take that a step further and think men are not necessary at all. This is Social Darwinism, pure and simple. All of us know the basic tenet of Darwinism ... the survival of the fittest! Social Darwinism takes this philosophy and maintains that those social groups that do not adapt fall away.

In Nazi Germany, abortion, euthanasia, and genocide were the tools used to see that only "the fittest" survived. Femaleists define social groups similarly, as either the *strong* or the *weak*. By redefining women as the stronger of the two genders, they are in effect calling for a new world order where women are the dominant gender and men are subjugated to their power structure. Legislation, propaganda, and education are their tools to accomplish this end. Many news stories, events, and even commercials are presented in ways that reinforce this agenda.

An example is the news coverage of the fantastic World Cup championship game in the summer of 1999 when the U.S. women's soccer team defeated China. Our family had followed this group of female athletes for some time, and our youngest daughter had even had the privilege of watching them perform in Europe a couple of summers before this victory. This group of athletes had trained gruelingly, and their coaches were superb. The results: They won a highly contested sports event. It was that simple: Training and coaching paid off.

But if you listened to Katie Couric or feminists, this was a victory of the greatest magnitude for the political movement, rather than a sports contest between two women's soccer teams. Fred Barnes wrote in an article entitled "Soccer Aside, Women Are (Still) Not Men," "Couric and the mainstream media became ideological ax-grinders and treated it as a political event with political winners and losers. The winners, according to the pundits, were feminists, the feminist agenda, Title IX, the women's movement, women with corporate ambitions, androgynous women, and little girls who will now be emboldened to give up their Barbies and play soccer. The losers were men. . . . In fact, the impression was left that women soccer players are better than men."[7]

How crazy is this? It is Scripture that gives women equality and dignity, not Social Darwinism! What is laughable about the feminists embracing this ideology is that Darwin was a sexist! Charles

Darwin wrote in his book *The Descent of Man*, under the subheading "Difference in the Mental Powers of the Two Sexes," "The chief distinction in the intellectual powers of the two sexes is shewn by man's attaining to a higher eminence, in whatever he takes up, than can woman—whether requiring deep thought, reason, or imagination, or merely the use of the senses and hands. . . .We may also infer ... [that] the average of mental power in man must be above that of woman."[8]

Haven't we come full circle? In the 1800s, women were protesting because they had no rights. Women now want to exhibit the same behavior that they thought was grossly unfair only a century ago! Femaleists have replaced male chauvinist pigs! Birds of a feather!

To accomplish this new world order, with its heavy emphasis on lesbianism, there are tragic results, including the death of same-sex friendships. Because our culture has given sexual overtones to everything, the concept of true friendship based on relationships between people of the same sex who share common interests has become uncomfortable.

Feminists have inserted themselves into every male domain, including the locker rooms of professional sports. Why do women have to be present when an athlete walks out of the shower? Former all-pro defensive end Reggie White spoke for many players when he said, "I oppose it. I oppose another woman being able to see my body as I'm comin' out of the shower."[9] In their attempt to break down the walls of discrimination in sports reporting, women have left pure common sense by the wayside, to say nothing of dignity and modesty.

Men can no longer have private social clubs because it is "discriminatory." Is a group of men meeting together to talk sports or play cards a threat to the feminist movement? Inserting a female into any male gathering entirely changes the dynamics of the conversation. I love meeting with female friends to laugh, feast on junk food, and discuss books and hobbies. Having a man present would change the openness of the conversation. Feminists object to men having the same opportunity because business deals are happening in these private clubs. This may be true, but I've seen many a business deal hatched by women under the same circumstances. Does this mean we have to outlaw any social club with same-sex members? How far do we take this? There is now a movement on college campuses to outlaw fraternities and sororities because they are not co-ed institutions. Is government now going to dictate who we can mingle with socially?

Why, when two men are in a restaurant or at a movie together, is it presumed that they are "a couple"? The only friendships that are "safe" anymore are those between a male and a female; otherwise a person may be suspected of being a latent homosexual. In fact, gay activists are going around the country rewriting history with the absolutely ludicrous argument that Abraham Lincoln was gay because he shared an apartment with another man before he was married.[10] Take that argument to its extreme, and you could argue that any two men who ever shared a dorm room in college, or an apartment to save on rent, or a tent on a camping trip, are gay! This is a tragedy in our culture for both genders because personal friendships based on mutual interests and similar personalities, with no sexual passion involved at all, can be one of the richest experiences in life.

I've observed a phenomenon among college students that exemplifies the confusion surrounding genuine friendship. There is a saying on college campuses that "so and so is G.U.G.," which means that they are "gay until graduation." Because of the sexual emphasis in our culture in all forms of media and entertainment, including daytime television and commercials about toothpaste, it is my belief that young people are so confused about roles that they will take a personal friendship and make it a homosexual relationship. The boundaries regarding the type of love one has for a friend cannot be distinguished between the type of love one has for a lover.

I think this is another sad result of the feminist propaganda against role definition. A young woman who enjoys sports, has lots of close girlfriends, and doesn't date much is told, "You're gay. You just don't know it." She may be as straight as they come, but same-sex friendships now carry another connotation.

This is precisely what happened to Amy, the young woman whom I described at the beginning of this chapter. She became involved in lesbianism in college when, as a former high school athlete, she made the decision to major in physical fitness. Many of her professors were lesbian, and she was encouraged to join their little community. She had felt so empty, so alienated from others because of her painful childhood, but this group of women gave her a sense of belonging ... an identity. She told a friend that she thought she might be lesbian, and that friend responded, "You know, I always thought you were." And that was that.

If you are a woman who admires another woman because of her brains, her beauty, or her wit, does that mean you are a latent homosexual? Absolutely not! We can admire a painting or a sunset or get a kick out of a novel because of the beauty we see or the skills and intelligence of the creator. And yet the lesbian mindset equates simple respect and emotion as sexual attraction.

Women who turn to lesbianism may do so for any number of complex reasons. It could be as whimsical as briefly participating in a fad on a college campus after taking a women's studies course, or as harsh as the brokenness that results from an abusive child/parent relationship. Although the homosexual community claims otherwise, there are no proven biological factors that cause a woman to become a lesbian. Counselors who work with women who have participated in lesbian behavior say that these patients often have poor self-images that may be a result of "labels" they have carried as far back as their childhood. How were they perceived by their families and friends? Were they accepted as feminine and valued and cherished for who they were as little girls? Or were impossible expectations placed on their shoulders that they could never hope to meet ... expectations that Super Woman would have a hard time accomplishing?

The most common form of trauma in lesbians is sexual abuse, according to Starla Allen and Patricia Allan, counselors with Exodus International, a ministry to recovering homosexuals: "Within Exodus circles, we have consistently seen that at least eighty percent of the women coming for help have experienced sexual trauma. More often than not, these women were sexually abused by someone they loved and trusted."[11] Wouldn't you be a little leery of a relationship with a man if you had been sexually abused repeatedly by men who supposedly loved you as a little girl? Your dad, your brother, a cousin? What about grandpa or your favorite coach at school?

One very important relationship in the life of every little girl—perhaps the most important—is the one she has with her father ... her daddy ... her papa. What if she just never measures up for the one person in all the world whom she really wants to please? What if dad controls mom with an iron fist, and mom is so weak-kneed that she never fights back? Would you want to grow up to be like mom ... or like dad? Would you be confused about which one you'd want to emulate?

It seems to be a rite of passage in our culture that all kids endure their fair share of teasing by classmates when they are growing up. Most are able to shake off the labels and the jests, but there are those sensitive few who never get over it. If you believe these tormenting remarks, if you carry them with you through your teen years and never see yourself as you truly are, then you may seek haven in a lesbian relationship ... often with another woman who has endured the same ridicule.

The message of the gospel is the answer for these women. This may sound incredibly simplistic, especially if you are a Christian who has homosexual desires. You may have prayed for years to be delivered from this struggle. If you are lesbian and are reading this book, I wish I could convey in the inadequacy of the written word how much God loves you and wants to carry this burden for you, His child. He cares for you infinitely more than any homosexual lover ever could. And the bottom line is that you never break God's laws; they always break you. One way or another, you will see the Lord face to face, either as His child or as His enemy. The choice belongs to each of us, including you.

A true love relationship is never an invasion. God will never invade our lives and force Himself upon us. He waits to be asked inside! "Behold, I stand at the door and knock; if anyone hears My voice and opens the door, I will come in to him and will dine with him, and he with Me" (Revelation 3:20). Much humor has been applied by the entertainment industry when it portrays old-fashioned tent revival meetings where an emotional evangelist asks folks to come forward, accept Jesus Christ as their Lord and Savior, and repent. What the evangelist or a minister is doing, however, is quite biblical … giving an invitation for men and women of their own free will to accept the presence of Jesus in their lives. It is an *invitation,* not an invasion.

God will let you go your own way until you invite Him to be a part of your life. But in exchange for His divine company, once you extend that invitation to Him, He asks that you yield your will to Christ, and leave your sins at His feet. This is repentance. You can no longer have your feet in both camps, saying "Yes, yes" to Jesus but continuing to mock what He did on the cross by living in a sexual relationship that He has made clear in His Word is sinful, whether homosexual or heterosexual. Sadly, most folks who are engaged in sexual sin find that turning away from it is an impossible price to pay. They aren't the only ones. The rich young ruler in Matthew 19:16-26 found that giving up his wealth was too great a price to pay as well.

A personal relationship with Jesus Christ is the most "freeing" experience in life. He opens up possibilities to each of us that we never thought would be imaginable this side of heaven. Jane Boyer, a former lesbian and now a speaker for Love Won Out conferences, says of lesbian relationships, "We don't have partners, we have prisoners." A personal relationship with Christ frees you from that prison and gives you the world. What would you rather have? Imprisonment or freedom?

If you take the Bible in its complete context, you know without a doubt that our God does not set people up to fail, even though at times it may feel that way to someone who is gay or lesbian. Homosexuals say that they cannot help engaging in same-gender sex because they were born that way; they would never have willingly made a choice that causes them such personal pain and anguish. But would God, who loves them more than they could ever imagine, set them up to fail because of something they could not control? Does He do that to the physically handicapped or to the retarded?

He is not an angry puppeteer who pulls the strings of people from heaven to see how miserable He can make their lives. He just doesn't operate that way. Psalm 103, one of the most beloved passages of Scripture, states repeatedly the compassion the Lord has on His creation. Satan sets people up to fail, not the Lord. Make no mistake: The power of evil can rule a life, but God is in the business of turning sinners into saints. Repentance does come at a cost, but look at the price Jesus paid for your soul. He gave up His life in your place.

If you know a woman who struggles with lesbianism, or if you are a homosexual, I would encourage you with all my heart to attend a Love Won Out conference sponsored by Focus on the Family.[12] If that is not possible, then my next suggestion is to read an excellent book by the same title authored by John and Anne Paulk, two individuals who were deeply immersed in the homosexual lifestyle.[13] Their story is too wonderful to do it the injustice of a paraphrase. However, their reflections on their experiences and their conversion to Christianity show that God is still in the business of performing miracles in personal lives.

Homosexuality opens up a door to evil that the Lord never wanted opened. The lifestyle is spiritually and emotionally dangerous and *incredibly* difficult to leave. Do you recall the Lord's words in Jeremiah 19:4-5 when referring to the practice of child sacrifice? God said, "They ... have built the high places of Baal to burn their sons in the fire as offerings to Baal, a thing which I never commanded or spoke of, *nor did it ever enter My mind*" (italics added). It is my feeling that these same words of anguish could be spoken today by our utterly pure, utterly holy Lord in seeing His creation buy into the lie that two women are a better love story than His divine design of one man and one woman.

We will never be successful in helping our homosexual friends leave the lifestyle unless we are balanced in the way that we present Christ to them. We have to model the divine love of Christ, balanced by His divine justice. We cannot be hypocrites in spewing a "sexual purity" message while we are engaging in our own set of sins in private. It breaks my heart every time scandal is associated with a Christian leader or church because of the damage it does to our ability to evangelize.

The lesbian/feminist crusade is a political/social movement made up of individuals. These individual women will never meet Jesus face to face unless we approach them with respect and mercy. Christians have an infinitely *better* movement for them to join ... the family of God. There is a way to model the love of Christ and still give a message of repentance. Too often, we give the message but don't model the love.

Christians are not the only ones at fault here: The homosexual community has often made open communication impossible. When a Christian leader expresses objections to its activist agenda, he or she is publicly denounced, ridiculed, and labeled homophobic.

This is simply not true. If the time comes when Christians are forbidden legally to talk about the issue of homosexuality as sexual sin, then we will have entered into censorship in this country. How would the American Civil Liberties Union like to have the Christian Church as a client for abuse of its civil rights?

We have a God who is actively involved in the lives of His creation. Again, consider Amy, the former staff member of NOW who left her lover, all the friends she had made after college, as well as a wonderful job she really enjoyed, to follow that quiet voice of the Lord. He has forgiven her sin, reclaimed her life from the pit, and she is serving Him with joy! But it hasn't always been easy.

She speaks frequently to groups of college kids, telling them about the lie they are being told by the lesbian activists on campus. Her tender message is how to witness to those who are caught up in a lifestyle that they might secretly ache to leave. But they are fearful because they feel such hostility from people outside of the movement, some who identify themselves as Christians.

Amy is also blessing the socks off of all of us who have the privilege of working with her day by day and seeing the Lord do incredible things in her life! She used to think that true freedom was loving whom she wanted, smoking and drinking what she wanted, and living the lifestyle she wanted. But she has found that *true* freedom is in a personal relationship with Jesus Christ, in experiencing His grace and love: "For He rescued us from the domain of darkness, and transferred us to the kingdom of His beloved Son, in whom we have redemption, the forgiveness of sins" (Colossians 1:13-14).

chapter 6

"What Can I Get for a Rib?"

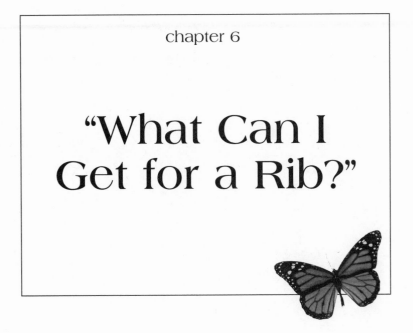

There's an old joke that goes something like this: Adam said to God, "What would it take to get me a gorgeous woman who will wait on me hand and foot, will be incredibly passionate, and is a gourmet cook?" God replied, "That'll cost you an arm and a leg." Adam thought for a minute and then said, "What can I get for a rib?"

Ever since time began, there has been ongoing banter between the sexes about roles and responsibilities. All of us laughed at the quote, "Women need men as much as a fish needs a bicycle." However, only feminists believed it! Men are absolutely essential in this world for any number of reasons, and to say otherwise is to challenge the divine Creator Himself.

Many Christian women are unsure of the honored role they have in God's design because of the confusion between their theology and the culture in which they live. A clear understanding of the distinction between men and women and their respective roles is not only essential to a proper understanding of God's design for life, but imperative for the Christian understanding of family. Christians aren't the only ones confused here: The Christian faith is frequently blamed for all sorts of nonsense based on popular public misperceptions of what the Church teaches.

"He who created them from the beginning made them male and female" (Matthew 19:4). From this flow inescapable "givens" inherent in the nature of sexuality itself: The attraction between a man and a woman that ultimately results in the consummation of sexual relations was all God-ordained. The functions of pregnancy, childbearing, nursing, and nurturing are biologically delegated to the female. Hard work ... right? However, Scripture assigns the male the greater responsibility: In his role as protector, he is commanded to lay down his life for his wife. Quite frankly, I like the role the Lord gave the woman a lot better than the one assigned to the male gender!

What an incredible privilege and honor to be able to create, carry, and nurture human life! The feminists pulled a dirty trick when they convinced our culture that becoming a professional working woman was more satisfying than being a mom. It went hand in hand with the philosophy that babies were only "unwanted human tissue," because if the value of child-bearing was denigrated, then being a wife and mom whose primary role was that of a homemaker was also devalued. Babies became an impediment to career goals!

Joyce Madelon Winslow wrote a very poignant article entitled "Is Life Really Just the End of the Line?" In it, she stated, "About 17% of U.S. women 40 to 44 years old have no children. I wonder how many of them, like me, once equated children with housework and dirty diapers, and career with excitement and travel—but now regret what they've missed."[1]

The passage of Scripture that is offensive to feminists is Ephesians 5:22-33 (NKJV):

> Wives, submit to your own husbands, as to the Lord. For the husband is head of the wife, as also Christ is head of the church; and He is the Savior of the body. Therefore, just as the church is subject to Christ, so let the wives be to their own husbands in everything. Husbands, love your wives, just as Christ also loved the church and gave Himself for her, that He might sanctify and cleanse her with the washing of water by the word, that He might present her to Himself a glorious church, not having spot or wrinkle or any such thing, but that she should be holy

and without blemish. So husbands ought to love their own wives as their own bodies; he who loves his wife loves himself. For no one ever hated his own flesh, but nourishes and cherishes it, just as the Lord does the church. For we are members of His body, of His flesh and of His bones. For this reason a man shall leave his father and mother and be joined to his wife, and the two shall become one flesh. This is a great mystery, but I speak concerning Christ and the church. Nevertheless let each one of you in particular so love his own wife as himself, and let the wife see that she respects her husband.

We live at a time when distinctions between masculine and feminine roles and characteristics have been blurred. This confusion in roles can be directly linked to the feminist movement and its impact on our culture. And many of us who are now in our fifties or older have been eyewitnesses to what has occurred. For example, four decades ago, "Mr. Mom" was a foreign concept, as was the phenomenon of a wife making more money in the workplace than her husband. The way men and women dressed was clearly distinct: I don't think my mother ever wore a pair of jeans. Homemakers wore housedresses and aprons, not sweats and T-shirts. Chivalry was alive and well, and men knew exactly what was expected of them when they were in the company of a lady. Watch reruns of *The Donna Reed Show* on television if you really want to see this vividly.

Female critics of the Christian faith point to the perceived unfairness of the leadership role God gave men in the home; in other words, patriarchy. But they fail to recognize the delicate balance given in Ephesians for this role. If the husband disrespects his wife, misinterprets the instructions in Scripture, then his role in the household can become tyrannical and oppressive. If the woman misunderstands her "submissive" role, the marriage can become one of chaotic insurrection. She may belittle her husband and defiantly grab onto the nearest feminist sympathizer, or at the other extreme, become a mousy weakling.

Scripture calls for man and wife, male and female, to serve each other, each valuing the other more than oneself. This is the essence of sacrificial love: that we respect one another *for the good of the other* . . . even when we don't particularly feel like doing so. It is really the ultimate accountability structure: the husband sacrificing for the good of his family and the wife exercising behavior that enhances and honors her husband. This balance in roles has never been understood by feminists. They interpret patriarchy as negatively as possible, picturing the wife as the doormat in the relationship. God never designed it that way.

In a marriage, the husband is to provide protection, leadership, and love, but nowhere is he given permission to disenfranchise or rob his wife of her personhood. Nor is he given the right to run roughshod over her opinions and feelings. He is to cherish his wife and to die for her if necessary. His example is Christ who loved the Church and gave Himself up for her (Ephesians 5:25). Ultimately, the husband is answerable to God for how he treats his wife.

In reacting against the abuses of male leadership, feminists have preached that all men are authoritarian chauvinists, which simply is not true. Just as every army needs a general, every business needs a leader who makes the ultimate, difficult decisions. Every household needs a leader, as well, and the Lord has decreed that this is the male's responsibility. Strong women may want to fight this until their dying breath, but my message to them is simply to get over it! Their battle is not with flesh and blood, but with the Author of Scripture, and they are not going to win! The Lord created woman to be most fulfilled when she is in proper relationship to Him and to her spouse. To fight His design is to guarantee that those women will be miserable.

It is ironic that the single moms I talk to every day yearn for male leadership in their homes to help with the tough decisions involved in child rearing. But many married women who claim to want an egalitarian relationship often struggle with their husbands for control of the reins. A surprising thing happens when a woman earnestly tries to understand and act on the Lord's instructions in Ephesians: Households run more smoothly, and marriage relationships are blessed. But there is chaos in homes where there is a power struggle over control.

My husband and I have two dear friends whose long-term marriage is characterized by their public bouts about who will be in control. The wife chastises her husband about the way he does the yard work, the weight he has gained as he has gotten older, and the fact that he is a workaholic. The husband retaliates by blowing up at his wife over trivial matters in an attempt to regain his self-respect. It is embarrassing to all who observe them verbally destroy each other.

Dr. James Dobson has often said that the basic need of a woman is to be loved, and the basic need of a man is to be respected. Check out that last verse in Ephesians, and you understand why this works; it is God's design.

When I was a social worker in Los Angeles County in the late 1960s, I had ample opportunity to see how poorly families functioned. Children failed to thrive in homes where the man was either absent or only an occasional figurehead. The welfare system benefited single moms because the family would not be eligible to receive a benefits check if the father was on the scene. We had an office joke that all the absent fathers were hiding under the beds during caseworker visits, but quite frankly, that was more truth than a joke. There was no place for an unmarried father in the inner city.

Because of the emphasis of the feminist movement on sexual freedom, single moms are now a cultural phenomenon not limited to those who are on the welfare rolls. What a price our culture has had to pay! Seventy-two percent of adolescent murderers grew up without a father.[2] Fatherless children are twice as likely to drop out of high school,[3] and 70 percent more likely to be expelled from school altogether.[4] And, perhaps most tragically, three of four teenage suicides occur in a home where one parent is absent.[5]

The stronger the woman becomes, the more of a wastrel the man becomes. Frankly, there is nothing quite so pitiful as a male figurehead whose female marriage partner has robbed him of his masculinity, his voice in decisions, and his role in the family. So often, these guys end up standing idle on street corners, or they take out their frustrations aggressively in every female relationship they have. There exists no balance, no knowledge or expectations about their roles.

I am not so naïve to suggest that all men *deserve* the respect that Ephesians demands. Some women make horrendous choices when they go to the altar. I am convinced that many of these women are aware, or at least suspicious, that they are tying the knot with someone who has deep-seated emotional problems, because these difficulties usually surface at one time or another during the courtship. However, many women do nothing to end the relationship before it is too late. I have seen this happen so often that I am firmly persuaded that some women, especially those who have more than one failed marriage, should never be allowed to select their next spouse, if there is one! To marry someone whom you know has real problems with women or with authority is masochistic, pure and simple.

Many other women approach the altar to accept the hand in marriage of a peach of a guy, only to be in for a real surprise years later. One of my dearest friends was married for twenty years to a man who led a double life as a homosexual, and she swears she had absolutely no knowledge of this. He was a well-known professor in a Christian seminary, and she taught in a Christian school. When he told her that he'd had homosexual liaisons during their entire marriage, it almost destroyed her. The pain was so terrible that she would crawl under her desk at work to cry her heart out, often several times a day. Their teenage son was horribly impacted because he not only had to deal with the breakup of his parents' marriage, but with an assault on his Christian faith and the way he viewed his relationships with masculine role models.

There are single moms raising families at the poverty level because the clown they married deserted the family. One of my daughter's best friends in preschool lived in a single-parent home. The professional ex-spouse had left the family for another woman while his wife was pregnant with twins and was caring for three other young children in the home! Human beings have always been flawed creatures! *Nevertheless, it was never God's intention that marriage would be an abusive relationship. When He ordained male leadership, it was for the nurture of the female ... meant for good, not for harm.*

Because man has been the protector and provider scripturally and traditionally, and the woman has had more of the nurturing role as embodied in motherhood, it was natural that these roles be set in cement culturally. Early feminists "thought outside of the box" when they talked about equality in the workplace. Although there are exceptions to every rule, I personally do not think that there was a vast male conspiracy to keep the female population barefoot and pregnant so that male dominance in the workplace would go unchallenged. Granted, there were definite inequalities in tasks assigned in the workplace, but most of our mothers did not have the college/career mind-think. Traditional roles were comfortable for both males and females. Moms who were homemakers enjoyed their roles for the most part and clearly understood how to make the most of them.

My mother was a phenomenal woman who channeled all of her gifts into making our home an interesting, welcoming, and exciting place. She went through phases that all of her children enjoyed as much as she did: We learned to dance when she went through her Polynesian music phase, and we tried to learn how to play the guitar when she went through her "Segovia" classical-guitar phase. She used her interests and unique giftedness in the home to influence her children in powerful ways.

Later in life, my mother joined the workforce in a casual way. But she was content in the role that society had carved out for her—raising children and being a loving support for her husband. If she had become a wife and mother thirty years after she did, she would have had choices available to her that would have impacted her children much differently.

One of my happiest memories of childhood was running home from school every day, *knowing* she would be in the front yard to welcome me and ask about the day. Around a family table we had incredible meals that took all day to prepare . . . homemade soups and rolls and pies my mother would not have made had she been in the workforce. Perhaps she missed out on some satisfying experiences, but if she had lived her life differently, my childhood would have changed as well.

God created woman with distinct qualities that make her as valuable as her male counterpart, but with a different role. Biblically, we are not second-class citizens, nor are we inferior. My parents' greatest gift to me was that they raised me to be self-confident about myself as a woman. They also taught me to be capable. They listened to me at the dinner table; my opinions and talents were respected as much as those of the adults present. And I was valued as a daughter. My mother knew her role was vitally important to the successful functioning of our home, and since her self-esteem was so intact, it rubbed off on everyone else. I think this is the reason I never went through the "burn the bra" stage that characterized the activist feminists in the late 60s and early 70s. I felt confident about who I was as a woman.

Perhaps this is one reason it was so easy for me to grasp the concept of who I was in Christ; since I always felt valued, I could understand the incredible love that Jesus felt toward me as a person.

I could understand the healthiness of a relationship with a loving heavenly Father because I had such a healthy relationship with my own dad. So many men and women grow up with such lousy self-images that the concept of a loving heavenly Father is very difficult to learn … but *not* impossible! Knowing who you are in Christ, and living this out in your role as a wife and mother, prevents you from ever becoming a "victim," which will be discussed in a later chapter.

Because the role of "family nurturer" placed women traditionally in the home, the feminist movement, as early as the mid-1960s, stressed that was the last place in the world a woman should want to be. If the homemaker role was to be debased, the role of the man as provider and protector also had to be dismantled. Men were touted as unnecessary, except for sexual purposes, and also mentally inferior. This, combined with the feminist viewpoint on sexual and reproductive freedom, spelled disaster for women. If men were freed from their protector/provider role, and sex was to be had for the asking, then long-term relationships were no longer necessary. Bed hopping became the rule of the game. Easily accessible birth control compounded the problem. A woman's body was not treasured; she was just another roll in the hay on just one more date. This has wreaked havoc on male/female relationships, not only in the workplace, but in marriage and dating as well.

I've hired and worked with hundreds of single men and women over the years, and I am particularly sensitive to their plight. Not only is there role/gender confusion, there is embarrassment about what they "hide in their hearts" concerning what they *really* want to do with their lives. The single men are embarrassed to say that they really do want to marry a virgin who has saved herself for her husband only and has said that her goal in life is to make him happy and bear his children. The single women are embarrassed to say that they really want to get married and have a family instead of a career.

I've worked with a specific gentleman at Focus on the Family for over a decade and have observed firsthand the impact the femi-nist movement had on his desire to marry. He attended college in northern California, and remembers when the radical feminists came on campus and disrupted not only student life, but his Inter-Varsity and church fellowships as well. He recalls vividly when the feminism movement really became the lesbian movement on his campus in the early 1980s. When the university proposed dismissal of the part-time, non-tenured "women's studies" professor who led the lesbian movement on campus, the lesbians shut down the cam-pus until the administration relented and kept her on the faculty.

This man felt that there was such anger projected against men that if women had been armed with machine guns, every male would have been taken out. He found that there was no longer such a thing as asking a woman out for coffee and a friendly conversa-tion without having all of his motives questioned. Innocent dia-logue disappeared between members of the opposite sex. He even-tually gave up, and rather than run the risk of being misunderstood or enduring false accusations, decided to not even ask a girl to lunch.

These problems continued well after his college years were over. He told me, "I was totally confused in adolescence and in my early twenties because I didn't know how I was supposed to act as a man. On one hand, I was told that if I opened the door for a woman or was a gentleman in any way, I was being condescending toward her. On the other hand, I was told that a man had to be more like a woman, but when I acted with sensitivity and compassion, I found this wasn't what they really wanted. When I would try to woo a girl, I would be accused of being too serious and not respecting her inde-pendence. So I would become passive, go out of my way to respect her space and wait for her to make the first move, and then watch the aggressive guy get her. I found that being like Alan Alda made me every girl's best friend and confessor, but John Wayne always got the girl."

The confusion also spilled over into the church in which he grew up. He watched his congregation move from prayer meetings to feminist liturgies that acknowledged "Mother God" and openly celebrated homosexuality. He said the church leadership was taken by surprise and didn't have the ammunition or strength to fight the change in culture. So they succumbed to it instead. Gender roles were omitted from traditional worship services, only gender-inclusive language was allowed from the pulpit, and the Bible became a cultural document no longer seen as relevant. Jesus was described so often in sentimental terms that "real men" had difficulty identifying with Him as a strong, masculine Savior.

This gentleman went on to attend a conservative, evangelical seminary, where the problem reoccurred all over again. When he arrived on campus, he was given a manual with clear instructions to use gender-neutral language on all class assignments, or the grade would be "Failure." The stickers on the door of a female professor who taught women's studies curriculum read: "Lesbian Rights Now" and "Not the Church, Not the State, Only I Will Decide My Fate." Announcements posted on the student opinion board boasted of mother god theology: Jesus might have been a woman.

According to researcher George Barna, this man's experience wasn't unique. We are now seeing the results of this feminization of mainstream denominations because the vast majority of men in this country do not go to church.[6] My friend concluded, with a touch of irony, that maybe those negative experiences in college, church, and seminary were what resulted in him waiting until he was in his late thirties to marry.

Another long-term male employee at Focus was part of the drug culture in college prior to his becoming a Christian in the late 70s. He stated that the women who bought into this culture thought that they had been liberated, but in actuality they were just being used. He said that he was so used to the strong female who was an "easy mark" that he never learned how to act around a nice girl. "I knew how to act with bold, straightforward women who were not Christians, but I didn't know how to act around Christian women. There was such role confusion. I was open to changing my behavior, but I didn't know what direction to go. Did I have to become 'more like a woman'? That seemed to be the assumption."

The feminist movement has been just as devastating to single women as to single men. One of the most beautiful women on my staff at Focus is in her early thirties and just now coming to the realization that she might never marry. She was raised by a father who treated her like a princess: "He took care of me, he treasured me, he opened doors for me." She says that the problem with dating today is that no one knows what role he or she is supposed to play. "The irony of the feminist movement is that the joke is on us: Men refuse to be men. They assume that they are supposed to follow the feminist mind-set. They are now used to being pursued by strong women rather than being the pursuers. That's what they've been taught. They almost seem scared. To act like a man takes courage, and it's almost easier to not do anything or have the woman take the first step than to woo somebody."

This young woman took a trip to Europe with her aunt and there observed an entirely different mind-set among men her age. She said that her friends were becoming attracted to men of other nationalities because those cultures treat wooing as an art form. It was her observation that in American society these days, two types of women seem to get married early: the ones who are so aggressive the guys don't stand a chance, and those who are really needy, who make guys feel that they are indispensable for their next breath. "Those in the middle, like me, are perceived as too self-sufficient. And if you're not married by the time you're thirty, guys think there is something wrong with you."

My conversation with this fellow staff member turned distressing when we talked about marriage:

People my age don't think love exists. It's just a fairy tale. If you're married, it's more like a business relationship that isn't supposed to last. You can expect only five to ten years with someone. We've all been exposed to too many marriages that failed. All I've ever wanted was to be a wife and mother, but I can't tell a guy that. Men have been trained to expect an equal partnership where the wife helps to bring home the bacon. If I say I want to be a wife and mother, then the perception is that I wouldn't be carrying my full load.

The philosophy that you deserve a fling before you marry exists even at Christian colleges, but for some men, the fling lasts forever. Men are not sure they want to be grown-up yet. Every guy I know wants freedom to ride his bike or do his own thing on the weekend instead of having responsibilities associated with a home and parenthood. There is no desire or willingness to commit to adult roles. To make a commitment to one person defines yourself because of whom you have chosen as your mate. But my generation is too independent to change its definition; it just wants to keep finding and redefining itself. To have a relationship, you have to give up part of yourself and be defined in partnership with another human being, and no one wants to do that. I've tried to explain this to my mom, but she doesn't understand.

This young woman stated that dating situations are awkward because the conversation always centers around career goals. "I would be frowned upon if I ever admitted on a date that all I've ever wanted to be was a wife and mother rather than have a career. If you are not on a career path, then you are not 'self-actualized.' Also, our society has equated relationship with sex, so if you are in even a simple dating relationship with a man, the sex question always comes into the picture."

The feminists are directly to blame for the change in perception for men. Our fathers and their fathers took seriously their roles as protector and provider. But read the language of the Statement of Purpose for NOW that was adopted at the organizing conference in Washington, D.C., October 29, 1966:

> We reject the current assumptions that a man must carry the sole burden of supporting himself, his wife, and family, and that a woman is automatically entitled to lifelong support by a man upon her marriage, or that marriage, home, and family are primarily a woman's world and responsibility—hers to dominate—his to support.[7]

This new mind-set, although it was written to "be enlightening" to women, has hurt mothers and homemakers tremendously. The truth of the matter is that women still carry the household responsibilities that they had traditionally, but they now have to have a full-time career to be considered as "carrying their weight." Children have lost out as well. Read another section of NOW's document:

> True equality of opportunity and freedom of choice for women requires such practical and possible innovations as a nationwide network of child-care centers which will make it unnecessary for women to retire completely from society until their children are grown.[8]

Do you understand what a message like that says to stay-at-home moms? They are perceived as "retired completely from society" as if they're invisible or don't exist. That message also implies that raising our next generation of moral citizens is not important! In other words, let's put all our rotten kids in child care for someone else to take care of so we can get a *real* job!

"If women had problems with male chauvinists in pre-feminist times, that's nothing compared to female problems with male feminists today," writes Suzanne Fields in *The Washington Times*. She claims that "the real victims of this mating change are teenagers, the never-married young adults on the lower socioeconomic scale and blacks of all ages, in all economic brackets."[9]

The above conversations with my staff members are far from unusual. My husband and I had a rule in our household that our daughters were not allowed to telephone boys. We wanted them to mirror the type of young woman that a man would want to pursue, rather than have them learn early on to be "aggressors" in male/female relationships. The mothers of boys at their school used to regale me with stories about girls hounding their sons by calling time after time in the evening, and I was always secretly pleased that my daughters weren't among them.

However, this rule impacted their social life dramatically. Our older daughter, who was the more sensitive, would say that she wasn't asked out as often as other girls because she wasn't in the aggressor role. Her reserved demeanor was interpreted as being "stuck-up." There is incredible social isolation for a young woman who is a virgin, who doesn't "sleep around," and isn't on the phone initiating the contact for a date.

What is so ironic is that the liberated, aggressive female today is the opposite role of what sells in movie theaters and bookstores, but try to explain that to any young woman who isn't dating! To illustrate, romance novels are best-sellers in every bookstore chain in the country. There are college night classes available that teach how to write such a novel, and there is a distinct formula to follow: boy meets girl; boy is wowed by girl; boy pursues girl; girl plays hard to get, but boy never gives up; boy gets girl in an all-consuming scene of passion; boy and girl marry and have adorable babies; boy loves his wife and their babies and is a devoted husband and father until death do them part. These novels are purchased by the thousands by educated, liberated women, and yet the story line is the exact opposite of that preached by feminists! Why? *Because women want to be courted, pursued, and protected by strong men!*

Just for the fun of it, one of the summer interns at Focus called the local Borders bookstore and asked what percentage of their total sales consisted of romance novels. The response was between 5 and 10 percent. That's huge! The light, romantic movies today all have the same plot as well: boy intentionally woos a girl and pursues her until she capitulates, and they live happily ever after!

Danielle Crittenden, the author of *What Our Mothers Didn't Tell Us: Why Happiness Eludes the Modern Woman*, has written: "When you look around at modern women's lives, I think few of us would be able to say confidently that the progress we've made has resulted in net gain. Yes, we are freer than any generation of women in history to hold positions of power in the workplace and in government; but this has come at the expense of power over our personal lives. I've heard many accomplished modern women complain—without irony—that they don't have the 'choices' their own mothers had."[10]

Crittenden has also written an article entitled "The Cost of Delaying Marriage," which I think every single young woman should read. In it she asserts that "it is men who have benefited most from women's determination to remain independent."[11] The sexual-freedom ideology that is the basis of feminism has been the greatest thing ever for a young man ... sex with no societal restraints, responsibility, or commitment! Suzanne Fields wrote in *The Washington Times:*

> Women may be responsible for changing the rules of cosmic consent between Venus and Mars, but men have taken advantage of their damsels in ascent. They've got

what they (some of them, anyway) wished for: liberation from the bondage of breadwinning. . . .When Venus begins to listen to the ticking of her biological clock, or worse, gets pregnant, Mars doesn't have to join the Foreign Legion to escape. He can just move on to a younger woman who isn't pregnant and whose clock isn't ticking. The guy won't be stigmatized by his male buddies or criticized by other women, either. . . . Does anyone wonder why male chauvinists have been replaced by male feminists? If the Titanic were to go down today, there would be no 'women [and children] first.' A male coward wouldn't have to wear a dress to get into the lifeboats. Some of the women would help him aboard. . . . As the female aggressively competes for the triumphs that used to be solely the province of the male, men are rediscovering the joys of hedonism. . . . Readership of [*Playboy*] magazine among college men is up 62 percent over the past four years.[12]

Isn't it interesting to note that thirty years after the feminist movement complained about women being treated like sex objects, television producers are targeting programs toward young males, such as professional wrestling, that portray women in degrading roles that are beyond anything the feminists could have dreamt up back then!

Many young men in this generation do not understand the protector role described in Scripture because they have been raised by mothers so indoctrinated by the feminists that it is a foreign concept. Their moms yearn for it, but they are at a loss about how to teach it to their sons. I was working at the office one Saturday, and a young man on our maintenance crew at Focus stopped by my office to chat. He excitedly told me about his college plans, but then admitted he was experiencing difficulty in a sociology course he was taking at the local state university. He said that the professor had polled the class of 200 students, and only five young men said they would interfere if they saw a young woman being raped.

Although this is appalling, consider the mind-set of the young men who have been indoctrinated by feminists while they were growing up with this message: Women are equal, women can take care of themselves, women who are caught in such a situation really don't mind because they enjoy sexual freedom. Contrast that with the protection the Lord has always afforded women in Scripture and His message about their bodies being holy ... temples of the living God ... and the role of mankind to protect womankind with their very lives.

To understand the Christian worldview regarding male and female roles, one has to stick closely to Scripture. Christian women often become confused because they take the feminist dogma they have been indoctrinated with and try to make Scripture bend to it instead of the other way around. I wrote down the following quote by Charles Spurgeon years ago, and I think it's a golden rule for Christians to follow:

> There is nothing so cutting as the Word of God. Keep to that. I believe also that one of the best ways of convincing men of error is not so much to denounce the error as to proclaim the truth more clearly. If a stick is very crooked, and you wish to prove that it is so, get a straight one, and quietly lay it down by its side, and when men look they will surely see the difference. The Word of God has a very keen edge about it.

Feminist ideology is more horizontal than vertical when referring to roles and relationships. If a Christian were making a list of her relationships in life, she would place them in a *vertical* list:

Relationship with God
Relationship with husband

Relationship with family
Relationship to profession or ministry

A feminist would write them on a *continuous line*, all having equal importance. A Christian woman would say that her relationship with God was the most important, followed by the relationship with her husband, followed by her family. If one's relationship is not right with God, then every other relationship that follows will be out of sync: "But seek first His kingdom and His righteousness, and all these things will be added to you" (Matthew 6:33). Because God's laws govern the universe, problems occur for Christians as well as nonbelievers when a job is given more importance than one's spouse or one's family.

It is easy for all of us to succumb to the popular, secular way of thinking about roles because of the ignorance we have of His order. Romans 3:10-11 speaks about this quite bluntly: "There is none righteous, not even one; There is none who understands; There is none who seeks for God." This is why discipline in the Christian life is so absolutely necessary. To constantly seek His face and to try to understand how He wants us to live, and then *do it* is not always easy. I heard Miles McPherson, pastor at New Horizon Christian Fellowship in San Diego, say in a sermon, "Kids do what they want to do; mature Christians do what they are supposed to do." God blesses us when we walk according to His Word, even if it is counter to culture.

George Gilder, author of *Men and Marriage*, stated in an interview with *Christianity Today*:

The church is right, and it should know it is right
and speak with authority. It should not allow itself to be
bullied by the media into abandoning its great patrimony,
the traditional values about sex and family. Too many
ministers pick up a copy of *The New York Times* or see an

episode of *Sixty Minutes* and assume the whole world is
transformed; and they think that in order to deal with it
they have to capitulate. . . .That is a terrible mistake,
because it betrays the church's purpose.[13]

One of the ways that extreme dysfunction is treated is for the
counselor to establish first with a patient what is *normal* behavior.
Our culture has lost the measuring stick to judge what is normal. If
everyone does their own thing, if what is right for you may not be
right for me, there is no way that young adults can agree on what is
appropriate in their relationship in marriage. Scripture is very definite on the subject, but it is no longer a reference point. Christian
women today need a refresher course as to what the Lord described
in Scripture as the truly virtuous woman, and that is contained in
Proverbs 31.

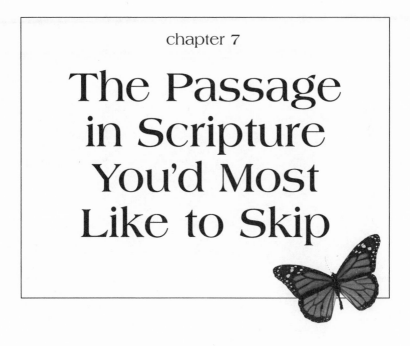

chapter 7

The Passage in Scripture You'd Most Like to Skip

The alarm clock goes off every morning at our house at 4:30. I have it programmed to the most obnoxious rock music station in our area because the sound will be so horrible that I can't wait to get out of bed to turn it off! When I look out the bedroom window, there isn't another light on the block, and yet far in the distance, I can see lights from the traffic on the interstate. I know there are thousands of others out there who are up, just as I am, with a bazillion things on their minds.

Single moms are getting ready for work before they wake their children to take them to child care. Women with handicapped children or spouses are preparing for the arduous task of getting them up, bathed, exercised, and fed before the day begins. Moms and dads are taking their showers before their teenagers use up all the hot water. Infants and toddlers are talking in their cribs, waking their parents and demanding attention hours before their moms and dads really want to get up. Others are dashing out the door to make it to the airport for an early morning flight. Farmers and ranchers are already taking care of their livestock. Middle-aged, menopausal women are on treadmills trying to recapture the figure of their youth. The world may look like it's still asleep, but it isn't.

Linda Evangelista, a top fashion model, was quoted recently as saying, "I don't wake up for less than $10,000 a day!"[1] Obviously, making money is her reason to rise and shine, but she has a choice when to set her alarm clock. The vast majority of human beings on planet Earth do not. For most of us, our days are spent taking care of the responsibilities we've inherited by being parents, or being employed, or dealing with friends and loved ones who have problems. That's reality. That's where we live.

There have been all sorts of reasons over the years why I've gotten out of bed in the morning, moaning and groaning and wishing for the comfort of my pillow for just another twenty minutes! I think the most difficult time was when I was a homemaker with young children. My time and my schedule were not my own, as any mom can testify. No matter how carefully a mother plans ahead, children have a way of superseding an "organized" agenda! Spilling breakfast on their school clothes, misplacing their homework assignments, forgetting they were supposed to bring cupcakes for the class until they are leaving the car at the curb; you name it ... all moms have experienced it. But one of the passages of Scripture that I have tried to model as a mom and later in the workforce, even when my patience has been tried to the limit, or I'm bone tired, is Proverbs 31.

Proverbs 31, also known among Christian women as the "guilt chapter," is something I could have chosen to delete from this book to make it "more positive" to many of my friends. However, it is impossible to ignore if one wants to confront feminists with a biblical model of femininity. So many of the passages in Proverbs talk about the evils that can be perpetuated by a woman, such as gossip and adultery. Men are as capable of these sins as women, but I believe the Lord points them out significantly because of our human nature: Our best attributes as women—our cunning, our verbal abilities, our perceptiveness and adaptability—can cause the greatest misery for others if we do not channel them properly.

My grandfather used to joke about the quilting bees held at my great-grandmother's house. A large quilting frame, suspended from the ceiling, was lowered, and all the women from church would sit around it sewing up a storm and "ruining reputations" while they gossiped. Verbosity gone bad!

Proverbs 31, beginning with verse 10 (NKJV), reads as follows:

Who can find a virtuous wife?
For her worth is far above rubies.
The heart of her husband safely trusts her;
So he will have no lack of gain.
She does him good and not evil
All the days of her life.
She seeks wool and flax,
And willingly works with her hands.
She is like the merchant ships,
She brings her food from afar.
She also rises while it is yet night,
And provides food for her household,
And a portion for her maidservants.
She considers a field and buys it;
From her profits she plants a vineyard.
She girds herself with strength,
And strengthens her arms.
She perceives that her merchandise is good,
And her lamp does not go out by night.
She stretches out her hands to the distaff,
And her hand holds the spindle.
She extends her hand to the poor,
Yes, she reaches out her hands to the needy.
She is not afraid of snow for her household,
For all her household is clothed with scarlet.
She makes tapestry for herself;
Her clothing is fine linen and purple.
Her husband is known in the gates,
When he sits among the elders of the land.
She makes linen garments and sells them,
And supplies sashes for the merchants.

Strength and honor are her clothing;
She shall rejoice in time to come.
She opens her mouth with wisdom,
And on her tongue is the law of kindness.
She watches over the ways of her household,
And does not eat the bread of idleness.
Her children rise up and call her blessed;
Her husband also, and he praises her:
"Many daughters have done well,
But you excel them all."
Charm is deceitful and beauty is passing,
But a woman who fears the Lord, she shall be praised.
Give her of the fruit of her hands,
And let her own works praise her in the gates.

This is a formula for success in the home and in the workplace! We don't know who this woman was, but we know how she lived her life. She was virtuous, resourceful, efficient, organized, energetic, and wise! And she achieved the praise that we all covet and cherish the most: that of our families, who know all of our idiosyncrasies and flaws! They know the *real* woman, not the public persona we show to the outside world. Our families know if we are hypocrites by simple observation alone: Do we speak one way when we are face to face with a neighbor and another way behind his or her back? Do we say one thing and do another?

When our children were small, my husband and I took them to Disneyland for the day. Our youngest daughter had just turned 4, and if I recall correctly, the admission price increased significantly at age 4. We were immature and broke, and we told the young man at the counter that our youngest was only 3, at which point, he looked at our oldest daughter and asked her the age of her sister! She replied truthfully, of course, and Paul and I were caught red-handed in front of our children. It ruined the day for us. Since that time, we have always tried to be entirely truthful with our children, behind the closed doors of our home as well as in public.

None of us succeed all the time in emulating the wonderful model given in this passage of Scripture, but the lives of those around us are enriched beyond measure when we strive to do so. This woman was *not* lazy, nor was she self-centered. She had time-management skills down pat. The passage notes that she awoke before dawn to begin her tasks, and this is still necessary for women today who run superb households. It is the only way to fit everything in that needs to be done.

Leaders of our women's ministry at Focus on the Family know firsthand that time management is a topic of concern for many Christian women because they've told us via questionnaires at our Renewing the Heart conferences. I learned my time-management skills at a mother's workshop I attended when I was a Girl Scout leader years ago. I later found out that the instructor was the wife of a Mormon bishop and the mother of eight children. She had her act together when it came to running her household. I adopted her daily routine, added my personal touches, and have run a tight ship since that time. I followed a systematic method in handling chores, defining by the day, week, and month when they had to be accomplished. I was always prepared for company, household emergencies, and those crazy times that occur in every family when any semblance of standard operation goes out the window.

But the skills did not come naturally to me, and because my mother had died by the time I had my children, I did not have her to turn to for guidance in running my home. To this day, I would rather do anything other than housework. I have always been more interested in gardening and activities outside the home rather than dusting and cleaning bathrooms until they sparkle, and I believe most women are in the same boat. However, a house has to be clean to be livable and sanitary, and there has to be food in the refrigerator, and pets need to be cared for, and on it goes. The time to do these things has to be part of the weekly routine.

The church I was attending at the time I had young children was silent on the subject of running a Proverbs 31 household, and no older women were assigned to the task of mentoring the young mothers in the congregation. I have come to believe most profoundly that older women in church have a key role to play, not only in mentoring the younger women, but in teaching Sunday school and Bible study. There is no room for Christian women to say, "Been there, done that! I'm retiring! It's someone else's turn now!" Retirement from Christian service is not an option that I find in Scripture.

It takes skill sets to be a Proverbs 31 woman, and those specific proficiencies have been eradicated from our education by feminists, who feel women should learn calculus rather than how to hem a pair of jeans or set a table properly. Don't get me wrong; my daughter is as competent a mathematician as her professor father, but it would have been wonderful if there had still been home economics courses available to supplement the skills I was trying to teach at home. If women who are mothers today do not possess those skills, the church needs to move in to meet this significant need. Possessing Proverbs 31 skills is necessary to make a house a home.

When my husband and I were house hunting in Colorado, we were shown dozens of residences by our realtor. I could tell immediately those dwellings that had a homemaker present as opposed to the ones that were just places to sleep at night. A house is a dwelling, but a home exudes an aroma, a fragrance of atmosphere, that beckons you to come in, sit down, and have a cup of coffee. In the vast majority of cases, the person who creates that wonderful sense of peace and welcome is the woman of the house, whether married or single.

My husband and I took a single woman who works with me

home from the airport not long ago, and she invited us in to see her small apartment. The minute she opened the door, we were entranced by her creativity and the charm of her home. She had created a wonderful environment on a limited budget. Many of the curtains she had made herself. She had skills at her disposal that compensated for not having a budget to afford a professional decorator, and she had made a nest for herself that was just a little slice of heaven. The point is this: Homemaking skills are as valid a high school or college course as any other field of study, and women should not feel ashamed if they are taking some of those instead of courses that are totally career-oriented.

Not long ago, I was walking through one of the departments at Focus. A young man was standing at a desk surrounded by three or four people, male and female. He had torn off the button on his jacket, and his friends were trying to tell him how to put it back on again. However, nobody there had ever replaced a button on a tailored jacket, so there was genuine puzzlement. I sat down and sewed on the button. I walked away thinking how ironic it was that these young people knew everything they needed to know professionally, but they didn't know how to sew on a button.

So many times young women at Focus ask me, "How in the world do you do it all?" My response is always the same: *"You will grow into it little by little, but it's absolutely essential to follow the game plan outlined in Proverbs 31."* The woman Solomon described was considered trustworthy by her family and community because she was hardworking, honest, wise, ran a wonderful home, reached out to others who were needy, and increased her family's resources by prudent investments and managing with excellence all that was placed in her care. Her physical attributes did not matter because her life was beautiful and touched everyone around her in a positive way. *Because she placed the Lord first,* she was balanced in everything else (Matthew 6:33).

This is precisely what gives a Christian woman the extra edge over a non-Christian woman, both of whom may run excellent households. I am firmly convinced that the woman who walks with the Lord has the advantage in wisdom, energy level, and ability to stretch time to fit all that needs to be accomplished. I can personally attest that the Holy Spirit has given answers to problems that I just wasn't smart enough to solve on my own. God has given me the energy to work late into the night to accomplish a task that needed to be done even though I was physically exhausted. I have personally seen Him stretch my days when I had too much to accomplish and not enough time to do it in. The Lord is the miracle worker for Christian women day in and day out if they only call upon His name and lean on Him for wisdom.

One time years ago when I was a young working mother, the Lord gave me wisdom I didn't possess, as well as time I didn't have. I had just been promoted to director of correspondence at Focus on the Family. I carefully orchestrated my work one day so that I could leave on time to make it to a doctor's appointment across town by 6:00 P.M. I knew that if I left the office precisely at 5:00, I would be on time for the appointment. At 4:15, Dr. Dobson called me and asked that I prepare a letter for him to go to a governor by express mail that afternoon. The letter was extremely delicate because it concerned the life of an elderly convict who was to be executed within the next several days.

This assignment would ordinarily have taken me many hours. We were still in the age of typewriters rather than computers, and my secretary was supposed to work only another half hour. I bowed my head, and with tears flowing down my cheeks, cried out to the Lord. I told Him that there was no way I could humanly do this assignment, and that not only was I going to be an incredible disappointment to my boss, but a man's life was in the balance. I was also upset that I would miss my long-awaited medical appointment.

The Lord took pity on me, reached down from heaven, and took over. My pen went so fast across the legal tablet that my handwriting was illegible. I had to rewrite every page so my secretary could type it as I went. The letter was in Dr. Dobson's hands by 5 o'clock, and he was amazed that it was precisely what he had asked for with no corrections necessary. Of course it was perfect . . . I didn't write it! The Holy Spirit touched me in my time of need, stretched my time, and the letter was dispensed. I also made it to my doctor's appointment on time. This is no fairy tale. I still get gooseflesh when I think of how the Lord met the need.

I think that Christians sometimes confuse "traditional" roles with what are truly biblical roles. For example, a husband with a green thumb may be married to a woman who trained as an accountant. It is logical that in their household, the husband has responsibility for the flower garden and house plants, and the woman pays the bills every month and manages the budget and taxes. Yet in some churches, this would be frowned upon because it is not "traditional." I can visualize the Proverbs 31 woman as being a whiz at math and handling the household budget. Therefore, I have no problem with a modern Christian couple defining their tasks in a way that complements their likes and dislikes, their strengths and weaknesses, as long as their *biblical* roles are not compromised.

My husband is a mathematician, but he intensely dislikes paying the bills every month, whereas I don't mind doing it in the least, since I am very "detail" oriented. On the other hand, I despise grocery shopping, whereas my husband gets a kick out of it. We have worked out our roles satisfactorily so that I usually pay the bills and he usually does the shopping. It works! It doesn't compromise his role as head of the household one bit.

Our vice president of Women's Ministries at Focus is married to a "Man's Man" who also happens to be a gourmet cook. She, on the other hand, has trouble boiling a hot dog. What would you rather go home to at night? Brajole with eggplant Parmesan or beans from a can?

A woman who runs a Proverbs 31 household plans ahead so that there are groceries and household supplies available in emergencies and bad weather conditions. Many Christian couples took precautions because of concerns related to Y2K, but this passage in Scripture shows that a Christian wife and mother bears the responsibility to make sure there are extra light bulbs in the house and other emergency provisions for her family as well as those in need at any time, not just at the turn of a new century (vv. 18 and 21).

Strategic planning is part of running a household. This could be as simple as always having the ingredients on hand in case a guest comes to dinner. We have become so used to stopping at the supermarket when we run out of milk or other daily essentials that emergency planning is not considered a necessary skill in this day and age. However, a prudent woman does this for her home just as she would have contingency plans for any emergencies associated with a job outside the home, such as the illness of a child-care provider.

It is my personal observation that Proverbs 31 women make excellent employees and are strong candidates for leadership positions. Managing a home and family requires the same skills valued by business. Show me a woman who has her act together at home, and I'll show you a wonderful employee. The things that will keep a woman from being a leader in the workplace are the same things that will keep her husband, if she has one, and children from calling her blessed.

When I was in college, I worked during Christmas break in a department store. One Christmas Eve, shortly before the store was closing, a woman dashed in with her three children in tow. She ran from rack to rack and threw items of clothing into her children's outstretched arms. She was so frenzied, her children became frightened and began to cry. At this point, she grabbed everything they were holding, threw the clothing on the floor, and told her children that they didn't deserve any presents for Christmas. The children were sobbing as they followed their mother, empty-handed, out of the store. All of us who were left behind were dumbfounded.

Although this is an extreme example, the chaos represented by this woman is not all that uncommon. She failed to plan for Christmas, she rushed to make up for lost time, and when her frenzied activity grated on others, her problem became their problem and the innocent were left holding the bag. This same scenario happens in business when a staff member fails to properly plan a project. Attempting to complete a complicated task at the last minute often affects co-workers, and the supervisor is left holding the bag. And women who have this problem with time management are often the ones who wonder why they are not promoted within an organization.

If a woman's home is a pigsty, it usually translates into disorganization at work if she has a job outside her home. I once employed an extremely bright woman who was never promoted because of the chaos involved with every project assigned to her. She gave a baby shower once for another staff member, and when we arrived at her house, it was a total disaster area. There was no place to sit for all the clutter. Her son spilled his plate of spaghetti on the floor during the party, and she rubbed her shoe over the mess, smearing the sauce into the carpet so it became one more stain among many. She bragged that she put her children to bed fully clothed so she wouldn't have to dress them in the morning. She never understood the contrast between chaos and order, and that order was valued in the workplace over chaos.

The Proverbs 31 woman was not a gossip. A woman shows that she can't be trusted if she is known as a telltale. If she communicates a lack of respect for her husband behind his back, she will more than likely communicate a lack of respect for her boss in his or her absence. The Lord lacks compassion for those who gossip against those in authority, as exemplified in Numbers 12 when

He disciplined Miriam with a whopping case of leprosy for her indiscretions.

Wishy-washy women don't have firm convictions. In the workplace, that type of behavior is exemplified in an employee who will never talk straight ... who will say one thing to me and another to someone else. It indicates duplicity. The Proverbs 31 woman "opens her mouth with wisdom, And on her tongue is the law of kindness" (v. 26).

Guilt is very common for women who feel they don't quite measure up to what it means to be a "Proverbs 31 Woman." I think our churches often play a role in the "guilt trip" because of the requirements and expectations demanded of women in congregations. There is a not-so-subtle message that often equates salvation with duty to church, and women find themselves leaving hearth and home to meet these expectations that often make their lives far more difficult.

Time with God does not necessarily translate into doing choir duty, Sunday school duty, Wednesday night Bible study, and so forth. These activities can be a blessing; my Bible study groups have meant more to me than any other activity I have done outside the home. But when they are mandatory and there is no flexibility, a woman can easily be overwhelmed and completely frazzled by the expectations placed upon her shoulders.

Verse 17 of Proverbs 31 indicates to me that this woman was probably in tip-top shape physically . . . in our day and age an aerobics nut! However, we've all been put together with different body types and temperaments. Some women can give 100 percent and still have the energy left at the end of the day to be at a church prayer meeting until 10 P.M., while others have only the wherewithal to get the family prepared to meet the next day. We need to stop putting fellow believers "in a box" and let them have the flexibility to serve the church in a way that is compatible with their physical strength and the other demands that come with raising a family.

I have witnessed, more times than I care to admit, an exhausted working woman leaving at the end of the day to pick up her equally exhausted children at day care, only to dash off to church for a three-hour choir practice. She looks as if she is at the end of her rope, and no wonder; it's like running a marathon every day of the week. There is no family time and no time to reconnect with that spouse who is just as tired. There is no chance for personal, reflective time with God, unless she is exceedingly hyperactive and can exist on three hours of sleep a night.

Christian women need to understand that their role as Proverbs 31 women is directly correlated to God's plan for their role in *history*. Millions of women existed on this planet before we were born, and we are living out our days during a specific time in history, just as our mothers and grandmothers did. When you consider the text of the Bible, from the beginning in Genesis to the end in Revelation, you know there is a plan for history as absolute as God's nature, starting with Creation and ending with Christ's return in glory. All that occurs between these two events has been orchestrated by God, including today's date on the calendar. The decision of whether or not we want to participate in His wonderful plan is our free-will choice.

We are all basically selfish beings, and we desperately want to believe that our lives matter and what we do individually will have an impact on our fellow man. God allows each of us to play some role for our time in history; a few of us might make the morning headlines. But for the vast majority, our roles are quiet ... behind the scenes ... obscure. The more I grow in my Christian walk, the more I realize that the success or impact I make as a Christian on those around me has very little to do with me and *everything* to do with God and His master plan. *Understanding this is key to understanding one's role as a woman in the course of history.*

There are so many opportunities during my day when I can be used by God to touch the life of another individual ... if I will let

Him use me. When I listen to His voice, amazing things happen. However, when I disregard that voice, He gives "the job" to someone else who is more receptive.

One morning, I was getting ready for work when the face of a new employee came to mind. While I was driving, I thought of her again. I knew she was a single mother, but nothing else about her. When I arrived in the office, I called our employee benevolence manager, who has the special job of helping staff members who have unusual needs. I asked her to keep her ears open about this new employee because I thought the Lord was trying to tell me she needed assistance of some kind. Since this single mom was new at Focus and had yet to receive her first paycheck, we decided to put some grocery certificates anonymously on her desk to help with food. We later found out that this woman had been too embarrassed to share with her new fellow workers that there was no food in her house, and that she and her children had had nothing to eat for two days!

This was an example of God working *through* His people to carry out His plans *for* His people. My role in the blessing was actually very small: I had only to listen, then act on what I thought the Lord was asking me to do.

When we truly understand our place in history and our unique relationship with the Creator as Proverbs 31 women, we come face to face with the fact that God's goal for our lives might not be that we are happy and content 24 hours a day. Compare our society's definition of happiness with Corrie ten Boom's experience in a Nazi concentration camp, as recounted in her moving book *The Hiding Place*. Would any of us have chosen imprisonment, extreme deprivation, and the horror of watching a dear sister die as a way in which to live out our role in history? And yet the Lord was glorified by Corrie's devotion to Him during these trials. As a result, women who were imprisoned with her came to know Him as their personal Savior.

We can begin to understand that the walk for a Christian woman is directly correlated to roles and responsibilities rather than selfish, materialistic, twenty-first-century "happiness" with a swimming pool in every yard and a credit card in every wallet. A mature Christian Proverbs 31 woman lives a life of service to others. Her activities are outwardly directed rather than being selfish in nature, even during periods of extreme pain. She shows who Christ is by her behavior and her reaction to adverse circumstances.

Our culture preaches a type of selfishness where one needs to get credit for everything one does or else it doesn't count. The apostle Paul suffered incredible hardship in a shipwreck and as a prisoner in chains, and yet he was at peace because he was in the service of the Lord. He didn't expect credit every time he did a good deed or won a soul because he knew the Lord saw everything he did, even those things he did in private.

We live in a culture based on personal fulfillment and happiness. When women are faced with hardship of one sort or another, they often draw conclusions about themselves and others that may or may not be warranted. Failure to advance at work may not be the fault of the male chauvinist boss, and misery in a marriage may not be the fault of one's husband. The feminist movement has told women that they are miserable because of the unfair treatment they historically have received as a gender, and that feminism has the answer about the cause as well as the answer to the misery. However, nothing is that simple, and their cause and effect are not consistent with the laws of the universe established by the Lord.

The Lord has made each of us unique, designed for a singular purpose ... to do something with our lives that shows who God is to His creation. Christian maturity occurs when one moves from selfish behavior to a life that emulates Christ. Some of us lead relatively uneventful lives, but reflect the Lord through everyday tasks, like assisting elderly neighbors with their yard work, being the mom

who is the magnet for every kid on the block after school, or show-
ing up on Sunday morning year after year to do those tasks that
everyone else in the congregation takes for granted. Other women
have more visible roles in God's "army," like Bible teacher and
speaker Kay Arthur, or Chairman of the National Day of Prayer
Shirley Dobson, or writer and speaker Anne Graham Lotz.

All of us have a role, and if we take our tasks seriously, it is the
ultimate, divine definition of feminism because we are known by
our love and service to others. And most importantly, we are leading lives that bring a smile to the face of the Lord. No matter what
our successes or failures as Proverbs 31 women, there is really nothing that bars God from loving us as much as He does. Sacrificial,
undeserved love is our inheritance as Christian women.

In addition to Proverbs 31, numerous examples in the Bible are
wonderful nuts-and-bolts lessons for women. Two biblical books
are named for women, Ruth and Esther. The mystery of the gospel
is that *strength comes through weakness*. The feminist movement
teaches the opposite, which is that strength comes through power.
Ruth and Esther were not operating through positions of strength,
yet God used them incredibly. History was impacted by the lives of
these two women in significant ways, but the Lord would have
used other women to accomplish His purposes if they had not been
obedient.

Both women were courageous and acted outside of their comfort zones. Place yourself in Ruth's shoes when Naomi urged her to
return to her people upon the death of her husband. How many of
us would have run home to our parents rather than stay with a
mother-in-law who whined and bemoaned her fate and was set on
returning to her own people in a strange land? Would you have
wanted to be selected as a wife for your physical beauty alone, as
Esther was? She was the original pin-up girl! Would you have been
willing to face death by approaching and challenging your hus-
band/king to save your people, as she did? These women's deeds

reflect loyalty, self-sacrifice, and obedience. Is this behavior that the feminists of today would teach in a college course?

Feminists have a distaste for Christianity because they feel it is patriarchal and homophobic. Some have rejected the authenticity of Scripture altogether, and others have attempted to edit it to make it more palatable to them. For example, there is ongoing controversy over the demands of feminists within the church for a gender-neutral version of the Bible, even if that means altering original text. Another example is feminist worship of a "mother god," which is not in the least scriptural. All sorts of mental gymnastics are necessary to pull off these manipulations of historic Church doctrine, and yet many women within mainline denominations have bought into the absurdities.

What is so ironic is that *Christianity has always elevated women!* "*There is neither Jew nor Greek, slave nor free, male nor female, for you are all one in Christ Jesus*" (Galatians 3:28, NIV). Christ had a unique relationship with women. He "connected" with them emotionally and spiritually. He elevated them … He took care of them … He talked to them … He understood them.

One of the most beautiful examples in Scripture concerns the relationship Jesus had with Mary Magdalene, the most "demonized" woman in the Bible. He restored her life by casting out seven demons, whose very existence must have been horrendous for her. Had she been plagued with convulsions, frothing at the mouth, violence? Would this be a woman you would want as your friend? Wouldn't she be someone whom you would go out of your way to ignore? Imagine coming face to face with the living God, who not only restored her, but granted her the incredible honor of being the first person He revealed Himself to after rising from the dead! Jesus met her at her lowest possible point where no one else would, and gave her a new life. He can do the same today.

Consider another example: All of us who have borne children can relate to the pity Jesus felt for the Syrophoenician woman in

Matthew 15. She approached Him, crying out for His mercy and healing of her daughter, who was cruelly demon possessed. The woman was so insistent that the disciples found her to be obnoxious, and they begged Jesus to send her away because her shouting was getting on their nerves. Jesus was so moved by her faith in Him, despite the fact that she wasn't Jewish, that He healed her daughter immediately. He understood her heart, her pain, and her love for her child when everyone else just thought she was incredibly annoying.

Any woman alive can feel gratefulness for the healing Christ bestowed on the woman who struggled with the world's worst menstrual cycle for twelve years. This miracle must have left everyone astounded because it is recorded in Matthew 9, Mark 5, and Luke 8. This event occurred before the invention of sanitary supplies, ladies, so you can picture how her hemorrhaging had impacted her life. Not only was she considered "unclean" within her culture, but the pain, smell, and discomfort that she endured is unimaginable to us with our modern prescriptions and medical care. The Lord could have walked away from her because she was unclean, and everyone would have justified it, including His disciples. Instead, He healed her. Jesus understood a woman's body and emotions.

Christ's tenderness toward the widow who gave sacrificially is one of my favorite passages in Scripture (see Mark 12 and Luke 21). This woman was more than likely overlooked by all the religious officials of the day because she was terribly poor. She had no standing in the temple or in the community. But she gave to the Lord's work out of her poverty rather than out of her surplus. Jesus said to His disciples that her gift meant more than the largess of the wealthy because she gave all that she had. This passage of the Bible reassures me that the Lord knows all that I do quietly behind the scenes as a mom, a wife, and an employee for which I will never get any "credit" while here on earth. My one hope is that this unseen service is pleasing to Him.

Look at the way Jesus handled the encounter with the Samaritan woman in John 4. He confronted her with her promiscuity, then elevated her by revealing that He was the Messiah. It's a wonderful lesson on how the Lord deals with sinners, as is the lesson contained in John 8 when He dealt with the adulteress. This woman had been caught in the act of adultery, which was punishable by stoning. She was brought to Jesus by the Scribes and Pharisees, and they were out for blood. The Lord confronted them with their own sin in this famous passage in Scripture: "He who is without sin among you, let him be the first to throw a stone at her" (John 8:7). He then quietly told the woman to leave and sin no more. True compassion and forgiveness are as available to us today as they were for that woman hundreds of years ago.

The comfort Jesus extended to Mary and Martha at the death of their brother, Lazarus, is another photograph of who Jesus was and His wonderful understanding of the nature of women. I can just imagine Martha thinking, "Good grief! Why didn't You show up when we needed You?" The Lord knew how much these two women loved their brother, and His timing is never our timing ... He is *never* too late in handling a problem ... even if that "problem" is a dead brother. One cannot help but fall in love with the Savior all over again when we study His graciousness in this story.

We have so much evidence in Scripture of a *risen Savior* who honors women, understands them emotionally and physically, and answers their prayers daily. The Virgin Mary called her son "Immanuel," which means "God with us." Say that several times in a row to see if you can grasp it! "God with us!" Say it when you are alone, or frightened, or in a strange place, or in an uncomfortable job, or in need of wisdom. God is with us, ladies! We could leave Earth on a rocket ship, and He would be there. We could go to the depths of the ocean in a submarine and He would still be there. He is alive, and *He is with us.* This is the wonder of Christianity, yet the religion of choice for many in Hollywood and the media is anything but Christian ... it simply isn't trendy enough!

Again I quote the *Good Housekeeping* article on Goldie Hawn, everybody's sweetheart: "A dedicated New Ager, Goldie has installed a shrine in her L.A. home, which she calls a 'sanctuary to house my spirit.' There, Goldie, who long ago incorporated meditation into her everyday life, is surrounded by crystals, prayer beads, and buddhas."[2] As a Christian, I have the power through prayer to talk to the Creator of the universe at any time of day or night, and to actually receive answers to those prayers. It is unbelievable to me, as to any other Christian, that anyone would exchange a *living God* for crystals, prayer beads, and idols.

Each of us lives in this culture, just as Esther lived in hers, "for such a time as this" (Esther 4:14). The battles may be different, but depravity has been alive and well since the fall in the Garden of Eden. I had a profoundly visual example of the coexistence of good and evil when visiting San Francisco one weekend with my husband. We had heard of a great little restaurant that served breakfast, and we decided to walk to it from our hotel.

We took a narrow street that had liquor stores and bars on one side and a church on the other. The side with the liquor establishments was filthy. Grown men were passed out on the sidewalk while others, in various stages of inebriation, were fondling one another. The stench of urine and vomit permeated the air. Obscenities were shouted to all who passed by. On the other side of the street, a dozen little girls were lined up in pristine white dresses waiting to enter the sanctuary for their First Communion. The sun was shining on them, which made their dresses appear even whiter. They were laughing and talking, and the sweet sounds of innocent childish prater joined in harmony with the sounds of the music coming from the door of the church.

There the Lord showed me visually that He always places His people *on the front lines* of a battle instead of on the sidelines. His church stood in the midst of human depravity, just as we are to stand in the midst of a culture gone crazy. The Lord gives us the strength, in our weakness, to preserve and make an impact for His kingdom. The gospel is the message of hope. Abolitionists needed courage in the early 1800s to speak out about slavery. Their message was not popular at that time, and they were probably as discouraged as Christian women are today in the abortion battle. But they eventually prevailed, as history has shown. When Jesus rose from the dead, He could have raised His voice and addressed the whole planet like a loud speaker. Instead, He chose twelve disciples to share the gospel, one person at a time.

One of my partners at work gave a devotion to our Executive Cabinet, and he said, "A student learns what a teacher knows, but a disciple becomes what a teacher is." The problem with human beings is that we try to figure out what God wants accomplished and then plow into it our way. We have to constantly remember that our role in history is to be available, to be disciples. We need to get out of our selfish day-to-day existence and get on board with the Lord's agenda.

We know that God has a divine plan for each of us in history. Your Proverbs 31 role may be to work behind the scenes in a hospital or crisis pregnancy center to combat abortion and euthanasia, or in your child's school as a volunteer, or as a professional in the workforce, or even as a witness in the beauty shop while you're having your hair done. The key to it all, in my opinion, is Matthew 5:16: "Let your light so shine before men, that they may see your good works and *glorify your Father* in heaven" (NKJ, italics added).

It's all about God and not about us! If you say to the Lord, "I'm totally Yours … use me," then *watch out!* You will be on the roller-coaster ride of a lifetime. He *never* ignores that prayer, if you are sincere and not holding something back from Him. Have you sought His guidance in following that plan in your life?

If you are confused about that role and burdened by the painful relationships you have with others, or if things are just not working at home, at church, at work, or with your extended family, then take these things to the Lord and soak them in prayer. After you have sought the direction of the Lord for your part in His battle plan, take a good look at your unique strengths and abilities. What do you do well that seems effortless to you but which seems to thrill those around you? You might have a natural gift with children, or you can make lemon meringue pies like nobody's business! My recommendation is that you use that unique gift to bless others and honor God. It's a good first step in the right direction.

Another positive step in the right direction would be to read and reread Proverbs 31. Reexamine the character traits of this godly woman, and then begin to make them your own.

chapter 8

The Battle of the Soccer Moms

For seventeen years, I have been involved in one way or another with handling the thousands of letters that arrive daily on the doorstep of Focus on the Family. I can say truthfully that nothing is as divisive between Christian women as the not-so-subtle war between mothers who have chosen to stay at home and those who have entered the workforce. These letters are not nice. The emotion could be compared to road rage!

Each side in this ongoing argument feels that it is "God's side" and that the opponent is not only sadly deceived, but a louse to boot! Both camps feel "beat up" and misunderstood by the other.

The battle is not over the question of whether or not women belong in the workforce. Because of the feminist movement, this is now a given! Women work! The two opponents leave single moms alone because they realize the reality of their situation economically. Quite simply, the two enemy camps are comprised of married women who have minor children. Their husbands are all in the workforce bringing home the bacon, either a few slices or the whole pig.

I understand the feelings on both sides of the aisle because I have been on both sides! When I was a stay-at-home mom with all the pressures that young children and a small income entail, I had a difficult time dealing with the glamorous creature sitting next to me in church in the knock-down-dead, gorgeous wardrobe and makeup. I was the one teaching her children in Vacation Bible School, and I was the one whose name was listed as an "emergency contact" on the health card at school when her child became ill and had to have someone come and pick him up. I was the one who provided after-school day care when the regular babysitter got sick, and I was the one who was the Scout leader and went on the overnight trips that the working parent was too tired to take.

It is very easy to feel contempt and jealousy when you think you are getting the short end of the stick. But no one forced me to do any of the above! I did it because I wanted to be an at-home mom with my small children, despite the financial sacrifices that entailed, and I wanted to be the school volunteer and I wanted to be the Sunday school teacher! I was able to schedule my time as I saw fit when I was a homemaker. It was as fun for me as for my children to be readily available for all the activities that a stay-at-home mom has the flexibility to do.

I never knew the other side of the story until I went to work myself. Then I became the one who was jealous of the stay-at-home mom who got to do fun things with my kids, who had the time to cook great dinners and bake cookies, and who got to go on wonderful camping trips, which I couldn't do because "I have to be at work in the morning." I suffered jealousy, pure and simple, when there was a school function during the day that I had to miss, but my friends were able to attend because they were not employed.

Some of my most painful moments as a mother were trying to fulfill all the expectations of my employer while balancing the activities of my children. I can remember being in a meeting that ran late, dashing to the parking lot as staff members were yelling questions at me, and arriving breathless at a soccer match, only to see my daughter leave the field after scoring four consecutive goals. I heard everyone else comment about her stellar performance, but I had missed it, and I spent the remainder of the game watching the children of other moms play ball. You cannot recapture moments like that ... ever.

My message to all Christian women, whether you have a career outside the home or are a homemaker, whether you have children or don't have children, is this: *Cut each other some slack!!!* We are so busy putting each other in boxes with impossible expectations that it's a wonder the Lord can use us for anything He needs done! The priorities of our lives are actually quite simple, when boiled down to their essence: We are to honor the Lord first and then we are to love and nurture our families. If you have made these your priorities, and the question regarding whether you should return to the workforce has been committed to the Lord *before* a decision is made, He *will* give you the wisdom you need about pursuing a career. He has promised this in Scripture: "If any of you lacks wisdom, let him ask of God, who gives to all generously and without reproach, and it will be given to him" (James 1:5).

The one thing that stay-at-home moms and career moms have in common is the same amount of time in a day ... 24 hours. Leon A. Danco, Ph.D., expressed it beautifully:

> In His wisdom God gives to each of us a limited, finite number of hours a year in which to achieve our goals, both material and spiritual. He gives us these hours in sequence, day by day, month by month. If they are wasted, however, they are neither repeatable nor refundable. He gives the same amount to the rich and to the poor, to the young and to the old. Whatever successes we may achieve in this life will come from the purpose to which we put God's priceless gift—time.[1]

Therefore, every woman has to set priorities in her life. Despite the message of the feminist movement that women are so remarkable that they can "do it all effortlessly," it's physically impossible to be all things to all people. The question everyone has to ask sooner or later is, "What am I willing to die for?" Is it a new car or your children? No one wants to look back on the decisions they've made in their lives and have a heart full of regret. Deciding to pursue a career if you are a mom, assuming you have a choice in the matter, takes on incredible proportions. It isn't a casual decision that can be reached independently of your husband or the Lord God Almighty.

I can remember the exact time and place when I prayed fervently to the Lord to use my life for His purposes. I was a homemaker with two young children, but I was also incredibly "hyperactive" for lack of a better description. The consummate "joiner," I was involved in every charity, church activity, and Bible study available. My children enjoyed accompanying me from meeting to meeting, church to charity, and back again. Our lives were never boring!

One day, I was sitting in the boardroom of a charity listening to two women fussing over what color to paint a nursery that would be used for blind infants. Since the babies would be unable to see the interior decorations, it was solely a battle of wills between these two wealthy matrons. My mind screamed, "What earthly good are you to the kingdom of God sitting here listening to these two women?" I closed my eyes and said a prayer that I felt with all my heart and soul: "Lord, use me for *Your* purposes. I don't want to do this anymore."

Several days later, I was with my two daughters at a private home for their weekly swimming lessons. Their teacher casually asked me if I had ever heard of the radio program with Dr. James Dobson called Focus on the Family. She had heard an advertisement on the air that morning for part-time writers, and she thought the position would be perfect for me! At that time, the ministry was located in Arcadia, California, just a hop, skip, and jump from my home by way of the freeway. To make a long story short, within two weeks of saying that silent, sincere prayer, I was working at Focus on the Family as a part-time correspondence assistant.

I had been on the job several weeks when I had to be alone in the office to "hold down the fort" while the rest of the staff was on holiday leave. I had an experience with the Lord that continues to give me gooseflesh every time I think about it. It was dusk, and outside there was a turbulent thunderstorm. I was cleaning up my desk, and I bowed my head in prayer to thank the Lord for giving me a position that I enjoyed with every fiber of my being ... one that was exactly perfect for my gifts. I heard the Lord say, as if He were in the room with me, "You are right where I want you to be."

Now I'm not any "spiritual giant," but I was totally committed to the Lord—heart, mind, and soul. He knew that and directed me to exactly where He wanted me to work. Granted, not everyone gets direct affirmation from the Lord in such a dramatic way, but it had a profound impact on me. I knew without a doubt that He had placed me at Focus, that He would be with my children the few hours I was away from home, and that He was using me for His purposes. What an incredible blessing!

If a married woman feels drawn to work outside the home, she needs to be certain this is God's will for her. I cannot stress strongly enough the importance of having your husband's affirmation of the decision because having outside employment will impact every aspect of your home life. The care and nurturing of your children *has to be the most significant* of the many things that need to be considered if you do decide to seek employment. If you have clear direction from the Lord, and if your husband concurs with the decision, and if you have excellent child care, then I think you can pursue a career and not be consumed by guilt that you are neglecting your family.

I know that my reentry into the workforce after a decade at home would never have been possible without the loving support of my husband. He was there to take care of the children when I couldn't be, he was able to work his schedule around the children's dismissal times from school, and he was always available to lend a hand around the house when I was overwhelmed. Looking back, I do not think I could have accomplished what I have in the workforce over the years if it had not been for Paul's support behind the scenes.

The Proverbs 31 woman did work outside the home, and was lauded for her abilities in caring for her family as well as for making investments and selling in the marketplace. Of course, she had maidservants for child care. Few of us can afford the luxury of having live-in household help or nannies. A recent study makes the child-care issue even more significant for young moms. *USA Today* did a cover story on research published in *Developmental Psychology* that indicates that, "The more hours a young child spends in child care, the less apt mom and child are to be attuned to each other."[2] The study found a "small but significant" link between a child being in day care up to three years of age and somewhat poorer mother-child interaction. Evidence like this cannot be ignored, even though we know intuitively that *mothering is vital.*

If you don't have peace that comes only from God about the decision to return to work, or if your husband has strong feelings that you remain at home while your children are young, or if your child care is average at best, I sincerely feel a mother needs to forget about the career path she wants to pursue and stay at home to raise those kids. No one will love them as much as you do except your heavenly Father. Stay-at-home advocates have a valid point when they say a mom's place is in the home when her children are young. I would take it a step further: Someone needs to be at home when the children become teens as well. They are capable of all sorts of mischief in an empty house. Children cannot raise themselves!

I think one of the issues the Church struggles with the most (and I am referring to congregations that collectively agree that a woman's place is in the home) is the issue of someone other than the mother providing child care. I struggle with this philosophy a bit. Who is more in God's will: the career woman who leaves her children with a babysitter eight hours a day, or the missionary who leaves her children at a mission school for six months at a time? What about the ardent church worker who is so involved in Bible study and other church-related activities that her kids are in the church nursery with a babysitter half the day and three nights a week? There can be very artificial definitions of who is a "good mother" and who is not. We need to get past these "rules" and be merciful toward one another, allowing these mothers, no matter what their choice, to be responsible to God, not us, for their decision.

Putting the child-care issue aside for a moment, I would have had no peace personally if my home had "suffered" when I returned to the workplace. Every woman is basically a "homemaker" when she becomes an adult, whether she is single or married, because we all have to live somewhere. I have always preferred the title *home-maker* (as opposed to *housewife*) because the female seems to be unusually gifted in bringing an atmosphere or fragrance to the home that makes it a special place to be for her family and friends. And again, the Proverbs 31 woman was lauded for running an exemplary home.

Granted, some men have a flair for decoration and atmosphere, but I can think of only two in my wide circle of friends. To a man, the everyday task of setting the table can mean simply pushing aside the newspapers so there's room to eat. To a woman, it means match-ing placemats and napkins, candles, or flowers. I decorate for every holiday that shows up on a Hallmark calendar, whereas my hus-band seldom knows what day it is! I have closets full of decorations that my daughters have come to expect and treasure at different times of the year. They wouldn't exist if my husband was in the "homemaker" role.

I realize not all women can or want to go to the lengths that I do. Still, the atmosphere of the home will ultimately reflect that woman's touch. Is supper "an event" rather than a nonverbal time of food consumption in front of a television set? Is your home an exciting place to be for your family? It takes enormous energy to achieve this "fragrance" in the home if you are physically gone eight to ten hours a day. What price are you willing to pay to pursue a career?

A homemaker should view her role as a *profession* just as if she were leaving the house every morning for a job outside the home. And our culture should value her professionalism as much as it values co-workers at the office. Sadly, the feminist movement has preached just the opposite, and women of an entire generation feel uneasy when they express their desire to be homemakers rather than professionals in the workplace. As a result, the skills necessary to be a homemaker have vanished from culture.

The obvious example is the family table. Meals are prepared in a rush and eaten in a rush, and the setting might not be in the home at all, but rather in a fast-food restaurant or parking lot. The skill set to make every supper time an experience to treasure leisurely, as was the case before television and the homemaker's return to the workforce, has gone by the wayside.

When you have had no training or direction on how to run a household, it can be overwhelming. It's often easy to let things "slide" when you are at home day after day, which is not possible when you have a profession with measurements in place to evaluate your job performance. So many times, homemakers are not given regular doses of encouragement. The fact that the toilets are sparkling clean or that there is a cake made from scratch on the kitchen counter is often taken for granted by the family. Your toddler may love you for reading to her for an hour, but society doesn't recognize that as an accomplishment to be rewarded with kudos. Are you going to lose your job as a mother if you don't clean the house one week?

I found that when I viewed my stay-at-home role as a profession rather than a temporary assignment until I could get on with a career, then my family began to view it differently as well. I set clear time management and performance goals for myself, and I can say without hesitation that it made the difference between an average home and one that ran superbly. I was also less "edgy" because I had my act together. My system involved a set of index cards that separated chores into three categories: those done daily, weekly, and monthly. This card system became so ingrained in my behavior, that after a while I tossed them, because I could accomplish it all by memory. After twenty years, I still divide up my household responsibilities in this fashion.

The Proverbs 31 woman ran a superb household. The church I attend has begun to assign "mentors" to young homemakers in the congregation so that the skills that have been learned by the older generation over years of practice and success can be passed along. Many young women today don't have cooking, cleaning, or sewing skills, simply because their mothers didn't have them and schools deleted the home economics curriculum. I believe this is a golden opportunity for the Church to impact its community. Christian moms can set the standard that is the envy of the rest of society!

One area in which stay-at-home moms excel is their volunteer efforts in the community. If we look at Proverbs 31:20, we realize this woman was deeply involved in charity work outside the home: "She extends her hand to the poor, Yes, she reaches out her hands to the needy" (NKJV). It is not only the impoverished who need volunteers to meet their needs. There are many ways women have impacted their churches, schools, and communities with their good works.

I have two extraordinary acquaintances who model the Proverbs 31 woman beautifully in this respect. Both of these friends are married to successful professionals who were away from home much of the time. They began to volunteer because they wanted to do something to help children, and to be involved in their own children's experiences outside the home.

One of these women began to teach at an inner-city mission school in Los Angeles. She would go outside of her comfort zone every day to work one-on-one with children who needed the extra attention far more than those kids in her neighborhood school. This was inconvenient in every sense of the word; simply battling the freeway traffic in Los Angeles every day to make the trek would cause some of the faint-hearted to shy away from this venture. Yet because of her Christian commitment to these children, she did this year in and year out with no expectation of praise or financial reward.

The other friend established groups that would help developmentally disabled children as well as gifted children. Her own child was disabled, and she wanted to make a difference in his educational opportunities. Her activities in the community would put any professional resumé to shame, and yet she has never sought the limelight or credit for her accomplishments. Colorado Springs would not be as wonderful a place to live if this woman had not made her imprint on it educationally and culturally. Her husband may have the "professional" reputation in town, but she has made her mark behind the scenes, and in many ways and areas that have more long-term significance.

Working moms have a set of new problems to deal with when they make the decision to pursue a career rather than remain at home. For many, the reasons are financial, particularly if they are single moms. However, many women return to work because they are gifted in unique ways that the Lord can use to impact their community and culture, which wouldn't be possible if they were full-time homemakers. These women are often the most guilt-ridden members of a congregation.

I have talked to countless numbers of these women who say that they have been ostracized by their church community because they chose not to remain home after the birth of their children, and furthermore, decided not to home school. They cry out, "What happened to freedom in Christ? My husband and I prayed about the decision, I have wonderful child care, and I feel the Lord's approval for my decision. However, no one will talk to me at church, and I have no place to turn because I have no church community. I'm a leper."

One of these women developed a pharmaceutical firm that was highly successful. Because of her business acumen, many Christian ministries were able to benefit financially from her success. The ministry that was accomplished because of her gifts has been incredible, yet her own church family failed to understand that.

I can remember speaking at a women's event at a local church, and observing the visible division between the homemakers who congregated together and the few working women who stood off to the side of the room. I felt their discomfort, but maybe a better description would be "shame." One of them said to me, "I'm never going to come to another women's event here because I always feel unwelcome because I work. I think sometimes I would be more readily accepted if I had sinned and had an affair rather than just returned to the workforce."

Another division among women in the church is growing in significance every year with the increasing popularity of the home-school movement. That separation is between stay-at-home moms who home school, and those who send their children to public or Christian school for their education. Again, this conflict is absolutely unnecessary, and truth be told, completely preposterous. My advice again, to every mom, is to cut each other some slack! Not every mother can or *should* home school her children! Is our Lord smiling on one set of moms and not the other? Did He shed more of His precious blood for one group than the other? Of course not!

The affirmation I felt from the Lord when I returned to the workforce in 1982 has carried me through the tough times, when I felt the disapproval of other parents about the choice I had made. I can say without hesitation that the Lord gave me the position at Focus, and I have tried to serve well and to His glory. I believe other Christian career women can attest to the same experience.

But I made several personal sacrifices when I did return to work, one of them being "spare time." Working mothers don't have extra time on their hands if they are going to run a smooth household, maintain a yard, cook family meals every evening, attend all their children's school functions, and help with homework. I gave up every club activity except one that I had been involved in as a homemaker. I also gave up my hobbies. My passion had been quilting, but I surrendered my quilting club and making quilts for almost two decades until my youngest child left for college. I had to set priorities as a working mom, and my relationship with God and my family had to come first. I could have tried to do it all, but my performance would have been mediocre at best. That wasn't acceptable to me.

I debated whether to share the following story with you for fear of being misunderstood. However, it illustrates the God-given differences between women. When my oldest daughter was in elementary school, I decided to go to my first PTA meeting. I have never felt so uncomfortable in my life, and I finally left early in a complete state of disinterest. I couldn't get excited about anything on the agenda, and the detailed discussion about decorating the auditorium for Back to School night almost did me in. I knew that PTA wasn't my thing from the get-go, yet some of my friends were very much involved in it and loved it! But place me in a business meeting at work, and I'm engaged and totally enthusiastic!

The same friends who enjoyed the PTA meetings at school would probably dislike the meetings I attend regularly at work; the detailed discussions we have about a piece of mail would suffocate them! In other words, we are all gifted in different ways, and we should rejoice and celebrate a God who made us so diverse, just as He made the wildflowers so unique! We needn't put each other in boxes with expectations that result in personal failure! Rather, we should all rejoice in the individual roles He has for our lives and in service in His kingdom.

We have a tendency as human beings to have certain expectations of everyone, even people we don't know! Church members sometimes create role expectations for the females in the congregation. Those expectations can be so lacking in flexibility that they drive a person away from Christ rather than toward Him.

God has given us all gifts. We are incredibly unique. When we use those gifts for His glory, whether as stay-at-home moms or career moms, the Kingdom grows, and we are better mothers because of it. If God had created all Marys and no Marthas, Jesus would never have had dinner! Martha's problem was a time-management issue, but let's face it; many of us will always emulate Martha more than Mary, and we could no more deny that fact than deny that we are female. *There is room in a church for both!*

All our life, our performance is measured. A pediatrician uses a certain set of criteria to measure how we develop as toddlers. When we enter grade school, the report cards begin. Every athletic team's success is measured by the win/loss ratio at the end of the season. And as adults, our performance in the workplace is measured by whether or not we have met a certain set of performance goals. That's life. Even churches engage in this type of evaluation: Success at being "seeker friendly" is measured by the number of new names on the visitor tally sheet, or the size of the Sunday school classes, or the number of baptisms recorded in the church register at the end of the month.

Do feminist spokeswomen ever measure how well they have achieved the goals of their movement? Let's take a look at the score sheet. In terms of employment opportunities for women, feminists have been highly successful. To counter the inequality that existed for generations, federal legislation exists that not only gives women the civil rights they needed, but gives them the protection of law in the workplace. These accomplishments were based on the premise that women were *victims* and therefore needed legal protection. The same premise was the basis of our labor-union movement as well as affirmative-action programs. People who had been victims were given federal protection as a class.

Eventually, however, if legislation is successful—if a social movement is triumphant—it should work itself out of existence. Once the barriers of job discrimination are removed, and women are given opportunities for advancement over similarly qualified males, parity in business roles should ultimately occur. It is my

belief that we are at that place now in this country, with a few exceptions. Women have come to a time in history when we are no longer victims, but equal in skill sets and abilities to our male counterparts. We are competing successfully with men in professional roles.

Women who have scaled the rungs of corporate success want to believe they did it because of their skills and what they deliver to the bottom line, and *not* because they had to be promoted because they were a victim of "white male privilege." Women want to believe they *earned* their promotions; otherwise, advancement is meaningless. It would be like winning the World Cup or the Super Bowl without practicing a day.

Unfortunately, the feminist movement continues to portray women as victims. This message is becoming increasingly annoying, especially for those who have made their mark as successful businesswomen. If women are victims, then the assumption would follow that the past 100 years of the movement have been less than successful. It is my personal observation that many of the feminist spokeswomen are writers, public speakers, and academics. I wonder how they would survive in corporate positions with enormous fiscal and personnel responsibilities. Having a "victim" mentality would be the last attribute that would make them effective.

I remember First Lady Barbara Bush often commenting that every candidate for president of the United States should have had the experience of having to meet a payroll. I would love to see every feminist activist who condemns corporate America have to meet a payroll. There is a time for them to put up or shut up.

Feminist Susan Isaacs has penned a book entitled *Brave Dames and Wimpettes*, in which she bemoans the wimpy attitude of some of today's feminine protagonists. Her first chapter is entitled "I Am Woman Hear Me Roar ... About How I've Been Abused, Misused, Violated, and Discriminated Against." She makes the case that too many women today accept as heroes women who are really wimps. "At her worst, the wimpette puts the blame for her

chapter 9

Victim or Victor?

failure on society, on men, on her mother."[1] She further states, "This canonization of female degradation and malaise is dangerous. It depreciates the suffering of women who truly are victims. It degrades women's views of themselves. Yet the mantle of victimization seems so chic that I expect to see it on the cover of *Vogue*."[2]

People who see themselves as victims do not assume responsibility for their behavior. What they do is always someone else's problem or fault. Sadly, Christians in the workplace are often as guilty of this behavior as their non-Christian co-workers. From Monday through Saturday, some Christians walk as the culture dictates. On Sunday, they go to church, hear a sermon, but never incorporate it into their weekday lifestyle or into their "Christian worldview." I have had the responsibility of overseeing the Human Resources area for many years. More often than I care to admit, a Christian employee will resort to nonsense that one would expect to see only in the life of someone who never had a personal relationship with the Lord.

I worked once with a female employee who made everybody's life miserable because she spread ill will wherever she went. Her immediate supervisor valued her skills so highly that he was willing to overlook her lousy attitude, but I don't think he ever realized how difficult she made it for the rest of us to come to work every day. No one could understand why she wasn't disciplined for her verbally abusive behavior toward her co-workers. Very negative rumors began to surface about her boss because of his failure to deal with this employee.

I was asked to convey the seriousness of the situation to him, and when I did, he was appalled and said he would talk to her. Guess what. She pulled the oldest female trick in the book, sobbing all over his shirt and emptying a box of tissue in the process. She blamed her troubles on everyone else, and then returned to her old nonsense. Many women will use their feminine wiles to their benefit in the workplace rather than *hear* what someone is trying to convey to them about their behavior. It's always somebody else's problem rather than their own. They're victims.

Male bosses are the worst at trying to deal with this type of victim behavior in women. I've tried to analyze this, as it is not the nature of most men to be bullied or to be manipulated in business. I think part of the reason lies at the feet of the feminist movement. Because of all the legislation in force to prevent sexual harassment in the workplace, a man is condemned if he ever uses his sexuality for personal gain. However, there are no holds barred for women. I have seen the most disciplined men become mush if female co-workers flirtatiously ask for their help on an assignment. All it takes is blinking those baby blues, or letting one tear trickle down the cheek, and men are goners.

All's fair in love and war, they say, but the women's movement has made it often more fair for the female gender than the male. Now some women will deny this vehemently, and they might even throw this book in the trash because they disagree so strongly with my words. But I'm speaking from years and years of observation and supervising vast numbers of people.

It has been a source of personal grief for me to witness the change in the workplace over the past two decades, which is now a hostile environment for the male gender. When instances of rape or physical abuse happen on the job, there are laws in place to prosecute the perpetrator. However, the stringency of the new sexual harassment legislation is not targeted at punishing crime, but punishing men. There is no such thing, any longer, as innocent male behavior.

University of Massachusetts Professor Daphne Patai has written a book entitled *Heterophobia*. She is quoted in *The Washington Times* as saying, "In sexual-harassment law, therefore, the 'authority of experience' has been given a place of honor. Such a move should have caused feminists everywhere to rejoice, for a fundamental tool of feminist analysis—the concept of subjective experience—was thereby elevated to law."[3] This is really quite profound and very scary. Sexual harassment is what a woman "feels" happened to her, but in reality may have nothing to do with what actually occurred.

The complaints I have observed from young women in the workplace against their male counterparts are, for the most part, lacking in substance. There is such confusion about gender roles that women are perplexed about their relationships with men. If a woman is unsure about her own sexuality or has had bitterness in her life, the law makes it quite easy to take it out on a male at work. If a man looks at a woman funny, or makes her feel uncomfortable, is that harassment? If a male says, "Good morning, Sunshine!" instead of "Good morning, Shirley," is that sexual harassment? These kinds of experiences produce complaints that are considered legitimate! What a colossal waste of time and money, not only for business, but for our court system as well.

Feminists have done more to harm the relationships between the sexes in the workplace than enhance them. But of course, this is their agenda. Feminist Catherine Comins stated, "Men who are unjustly accused of rape can sometimes gain from the experience."[4] Since when is it justifiable to destroy a person's reputation, no matter what gender? It's ironic that feminists want all the good things that they perceive males have traditionally had in and outside the workplace, but the ladies hate the object of their affection! Does that make sense? Again, they're adding two and two and getting five for an answer.

Years ago, I supervised a lovely young woman who fell desperately in love with one of the men in the office. They were inseparable during their breaks ... whispering, hand-holding, and kissing when they thought no one was looking. After several months, she decided she wanted to date other gentlemen, which devastated the young man. He would come to her desk to try to convince her to eat lunch with him, send love notes to her, and wait after work to walk her to her car. She never wanted to completely break it off with him, but rather keep him in her "back pocket" until she was done playing the field ... rather like a spare tire.

One day, she came to me to file a sexual harassment complaint against him because she had found someone else, and she no longer wanted his attention. In other words, she wanted her employer to break off the relationship because she didn't have the courage to do so herself. This is an example of a totally inappropriate sexual harassment accusation. If I had not known the circumstances, the young man's career and reputation could have been seriously damaged.

It is my observation that men who are truly "predators" in the workplace will usually pick as their victim a very sensitive, gentle woman who has the tendency to think the best of every person she ever meets. This type of woman has a great deal of difficulty believing that someone in authority would ever take advantage of her, so when the danger signals began to occur, she ignores them or absorbs the "bad feeling" that comes with the improper advance as being her fault in some way. Again, discernment is necessary here, because a male co-worker putting his arm around a woman in a brief hug might be innocently trying only to show moral support.

My advice to those of you who may be such women is to seek the counsel of a *mature* female, preferably one who is happily married or who has sons, to confidentially share and validate your concerns if you feel there are red flags about a male co-worker's behavior. This should be the first step a woman takes, prior to filing any type of formal sexual harassment complaint.

The second step should be to ask yourself if you ever did anything to encourage the inappropriate behavior: Did you set boundaries for yourself? Did you directly tell the male offender that you did not like what he was doing? Subtle language does not work with men; they don't get it. Did you shyly smile, inadvertently giving encouragement, the first time he touched you? Did you join in the repartee when dirty jokes or suggestive language was bantered at lunch? Did you sympathize when the man began to tell you his problems with his wife or girlfriend in such a way that he looked at you as a potential "new relationship"? Did you take control of the situation rather than letting it control you?

It is incumbent that a woman not accuse a male co-worker of sexual harassment unless her response to the inappropriate behavior has been above reproach. Otherwise, she has participated in the harassment, whether unwittingly or not, and has set the male co-worker up "to fail." Again, and I cannot stress this too strongly, men don't do well with nuances in language. *Very direct communication* is always best when you are dealing with them.

Allow me to illustrate: A close friend came to me recently and tearfully admitted that she had gone to the employee relations manager at her place of employment and filed a sexual harassment complaint against her male supervisor. She was terribly distraught, and when I questioned her, said that she was beginning to regret her actions. She admitted that she had "spilled her guts" to this man in confidence by revealing her deepest sexual fantasies, and his crude verbal response upset her.

She did not receive the sympathy from me she expected. I told her she should never have confided such thoughts to a male co-worker, much less her boss. And she had no business filing a harassment complaint against him simply because she was angry about the way he responded to her inappropriate revelations. She had initiated the incident, not her supervisor.

Character assassination is inexcusable in cases like this. However, bona fide sexual harassment is inexcusable as well, whether in the workplace or in a social setting. A woman should never hesitate to file a complaint that is legitimate.

In defending men in the workplace, I am not discounting the fact that some male co-workers are absolute predators, for lack of a better description. I've worked with a number of them over the years, most often in the secular world. (How many of you have worked for a boss who was your best friend when your work made him look like a genius? But when the first mistake occurred, he acted as if he never knew you.)

However, this chapter is addressing female offenders, not male! Too often, women use their natural charm, verbal skills, and even tears to get their way, whether on a date, at home, or in the workplace. When they do this, it is no longer a level playing field because they are accomplishing their ends by being victims rather than honorable opponents. And women will *never* have the right to be considered equal to men in the workplace if they continue to play the victim or use feminine manipulation to work their way up the corporate ladder.

One of my favorite people at Focus supervises over one third of the workforce. I asked him one day what bothered him most about dealing with female employees, if anything. At first he said that nothing bothered him …that he had absolutely wonderful working relationships with all the women on his staff. Then followed thirty minutes of, as Paul Harvey would say, "the rest of the story."

He stated that he always felt constrained to be honest and direct over a business issue, as he would be with another man, because "I have to make it an *emotional feeling* issue in order to address it. I can't deal bluntly with the issue and move on. And I can't go to one woman to deal with a professional issue because she makes it the business of her whole group of friends and co-workers; they all become the 'victim.' So then I have to assure the entire group that they are not bad just to get a change for the better in one person. When I do address an issue one-on-one, the lady runs to her friends to share about the confrontation, and then asks for their prayer support to get through it, thus making me the bad guy and exonerating her from responsibility."

Again, this is the victim mindset among women in the workplace. It is very tedious to deal with because of the lack of responsibility it engenders. I have always found it easier to communicate with men than women when I need to confront bad behavior, because the conversation is direct and to the point. The tendency of women to bring their emotions, as well as those of their compatriots, into every situation is exceedingly tiresome for those in positions of authority.

Men like working with *feminine* women who are straightforward, even blunt. Female-to-male communication should not be a foreign language! Women somehow think that anyone can read their minds, but this simply isn't so. Beating around the bush doesn't work in a marriage, or in talking with a friend, so why do women think it should work in the workplace? Men don't like to be in the position of guessing what a woman is really saying. If there is a difference of opinion, two men will logically talk it through with little emotion other than their natural inclination to be competitive. I cannot tell you the number of times I have heard male managers lament that they often give the wrong impression to females who work with them. They may appear brusque and unapproachable by staff simply because they don't have the time to listen to a long-winded debriefing by a female who never quite gets to the point.

One gentleman resorted to taking an egg timer out of his desk drawer when one of his editors came in for a debriefing because it was the only way he could keep her to under an hour. This was completely disrespectful on his part, and yet the employee was equally disrespectful in not coming to a meeting prepared to give a succinct report. This type of situation often ends up in employee relations as a "victim" or "sexual harassment" complaint.

The salary structure of most companies is based on formulas that award increases based on the level of responsibility one carries. In other words, the only way to move up the salary ladder is to go after positions with more authority, which are fewer in number than entry level positions. Feminists have convinced women that what satisfies a man is what should satisfy a woman as well, so the competition to advance at work is the goal that both sexes pursue.

As I mentioned in chapter 6, single career women are *often* asked on a date what they perceive as their career path. They are told that staying in the same job year after year is not the right answer because it denotes that they lack motivation, even if they happen to love the job and it fits them to a T! But God's economy is not the world's economy, and when you are sold out to a life of Christian service, job title and salary come to mean less and less.

The vast majority of young women I have known who entered the workplace immediately after completing their education have as their goal a move up the corporate ladder to a position of authority or leadership. This defines success for them. I have often challenged the women who come to me for advice on how to advance into leadership to search their hearts to see if this is what they *really* want. It is so easy to buy into the feminist mind-set. Instead, *ask the Lord what He wants you to do with your life.* It may sound simple, but it is truth: God will place you exactly where He wants you to be if you surrender your life to Him.

That might not be in the professional working world or in a position of leadership. Three of my former staff members are now on the mission field because they followed God's career path for their lives. The woman who headed up our Renewing the Heart conferences left a very successful law practice to come to Focus on the Family to work for substantially less money because of the Lord's leading. Feminist formulas don't work for Christians who are *committed* to God's work—God's way.

One of our receptionists at Focus has such a Christ-like attitude in the way that she relates to her co-workers that her story bears mentioning here. She had a wonderful position as a secretary in an elementary school, and she loved her job dearly. The teachers and students cherished her as well; she was a "refuge" for the faculty when they were distressed or harried, and a safe haven for a child with an upset tummy. She began to experience some friction with the other secretary in the office, as well as the principal, but she couldn't understand why. She felt she was doing an excellent job.

One day she had a long discussion with the principal, and for the first time she discovered that his perception of her work responsibilities was different from hers. He wanted a "detail" person in the front office, and he valued clerical skills more than her people skills. This woman went home, committed the matter to prayer, and made the decision to deal herself out of the job rather than cause the other secretary and the principal more grief. She said to me with tears in her eyes that she felt as if she had lost a limb because she had given up something she loved so much. But then the Lord brought her to Focus, where her people skills were *exactly* what we needed desperately! She said, "I can truly say God wanted me here instead of the other job."

I have rarely observed women with a "victim" mentality progress into leadership roles. The Lord seems to bring women to the forefront who have been faithful in fulfilling the little tasks that might be invisible to everyone around them. Sometimes He chooses the most unlikely people, those who have been content to remain in the background rather than aggressively seek a larger role. At a time when women were regarded as second-class citizens, God chose Deborah to lead. She was such an unlikely choice: a former housewife calling the shots in battle for her nation! When you show yourself faithful in the small things, then it follows that you will be faithful with larger responsibilities. If you honor God when you are in an obscure position, then God will honor you when He needs you in a public position:

Brothers, think of what you were when you were called. Not many of you were wise by human standards; not many were influential; not many were of noble birth. But God chose the foolish things of the world to shame the wise; God chose the weak things of the world to shame the strong. He chose the lowly things of this world and the despised things—and the things that are not—to

nullify the things that are, so that no one may boast
before him. It is because of him that you are in Christ
Jesus, who has become for us wisdom from God—that is,
our righteousness, holiness and redemption. Therefore, as
it is written: "Let him who boasts boast in the Lord."
(1 Corinthians 1:26-31, NIV)

A Christian group called Priority Associates recently polled its
members, all professional career women, to get a take on the chal-
lenges they face in the workplace. One of the questions asked was what
character traits they valued in their co-workers. The number-one character trait was honesty, followed by integrity and loyalty.[5] This is not
surprising; every one of us would like these traits present in the people
we deal with, whether or not we work outside the home. These same
traits were perfectly modeled by Christ when He became man.

A Christian woman should be an archetype of excellence in the
workplace! She should model femininity, industry, and discretion.
Her relationships with her male and female co-workers should
model respect. Her language should be straightforward and pure.
She should never make excuses, but should assume responsibility
for her behavior, including the mistakes she makes. This translates
into the ideal employee, no matter where one works. And it also
translates into *incredible Christian witness.*

Let us turn the corner and look at women as victims in a social
context other than the work force. Yes, there are *true* victims out
there: little girls who have been molested by trusted family members;
women in abusive marriages; young college students who have been
traumatized by date rape. Nothing can trivialize what they have
experienced.

One of my friends is hiding from her husband, and has been
for the past three years. She was introduced to him in a church setting, and she describes him as "the most charming man I have ever
met." He identified himself as a Christian, and his parents had

impeccable credentials within the church. However, within one week after saying "I do," Dr. Jekyll became Mr. Hyde, and for four years my friend lived a nightmare.

This scenario is actually quite common among women who have lived with abusive husbands. They will say that their spouse was incredibly romantic when they were in the "honeymoon" phase of the relationship. This is one reason that marriage and family counselors will always stress the importance of a long courtship. Anyone can perform well for six months ... but two years?

Another friend at work married two losers. Both had addiction problems with drugs and alcohol, and one of her husbands sexually abused her daughter when she was a toddler. When she left each marriage, her family and friends told her that these crazy liaisons were not her fault; her husbands were complete idiots. Before her second separation, she realized this: "There were so many things wrong with them that I felt like a saint. But then I had to confront my choices and ask God what was wrong with *me*. The Lord showed me that I was secure with unhealthiness. When I was around healthy men, I felt insecure and uninterested. I felt control when I was the one 'fixing' another person."

Both of these women could have bathed themselves in an ocean of sympathy from friends and co-workers. However, they have done exactly the opposite. Neither one perceives herself as a victim, but rather as a victor through her faith in Christ. Both women know firsthand how He is able to redeem a life from the pit. One of them wrote to me, "I know this sounds like a simple answer, but this is really what it all boils down to. I am never alone, I am always loved and accepted, I am always comforted, I am always forgiven, I am never betrayed, and I will never be left or forsaken. He has promised me this, and He always keeps His promises."

Christianity is a mystery to feminists; it simply doesn't make sense as a worldview! Who was more abused by His fellow man than Jesus? He had every reason to fight back and *destroy* those who

hung Him on a cross to die. Why didn't He pit His anger against
the patriarchal Church leadership? He was a victim, for goodness'
sake! They took away His civil rights—*His life!*

And yet the mystery of the gospel is that when you have a personal relationship with Christ, *He encourages you not to be a victim.*
He will eventually deal with the abuser more harshly than you ever
could. He is your advocate. No one has any power over you whatsoever if you have the Lord. This is a difficult concept to understand
and incorporate into your life if you have the mentality of a victim.

Many Christian women who are in abusive relationships become
confused over what the Bible teaches regarding the sanctity of marriage. They will endure years of abuse claiming the message of 1
Corinthians 13:7, which teaches that love bears all things, believes all
things, hopes all things, and endures all things. However, God never
contradicts Himself in Scripture, and husbands who abuse their wives
clearly defy the definition of their role given in Ephesians 5. Look
deeply at the character of the Lord revealed through Scripture: Would
He ever condemn one of His children to years of physical abuse?

Women who have been abused have difficulty understanding
the *nobility* of their human soul ... the incredibly unique person the
Lord created and knew before conception even occurred. Psalm
139:15-16 states this so beautifully:

> My frame was not hidden from You,
> When I was made in secret,
> And skillfully wrought in the depths of the earth;
> Your eyes have seen my unformed substance;
> And in Your book were all written
> The days that were ordained for me,
> When as yet there was not one of them.

These women may never incorporate into their self-image the
concept that they became royalty when they became God's children,

the special daughters for whom Jesus went to the Cross and shed His blood to redeem them. Instead, they will believe what their spouses say they are, the lie that "legitimizes" the abuse they suffer.

Does this mean that you will never be abused if you are a Christian woman who does understand who you are in the eyes of Christ? Certainly not. Lousy things happen all the time to God's people, usually because we have made bad decisions for our lives and in our personal relationships. But He gives us the power and the resources to leave horrible situations, and He has promised in His Word that He will take care of us. Feminists say you are still a victim, but Jesus says, "I have made you the victor; you belong to Me."

If you believe that you are a victim, others will treat you as a victim, and you will never make good choices for your life. How many times do women who were abused as little girls pick as their husband the same type of man as the abuser? I saw this countless times when I was a caseworker. If you accept the feminist message that women are victims and powerless, you will always be the loser. Women are *not* powerless, and you are believing a lie if you think they are. You also mock God, who will always be the vindicator of the weak.

When I was a social worker, one of my clients was married to a terribly abusive man. During my visits, he would try to intimidate me. Even though I was "jello" inside, I put on a tough exterior. He once answered the door completely naked, and when I didn't react, he came forward with his fist raised. As I backed out toward my car, he followed in pursuit, keeping his arm raised. I never screamed ... I didn't want to give him the satisfaction of knowing I was scared spitless. I could have cried and begged and pleaded, but I didn't. When I got to my car, he lowered his arm and started to laugh. It was the beginning of a weird relationship: He actually allowed me in the home to work with his family.

I learned a valuable lesson: Bullies will taunt only those who don't stand up to them. Again, this concept is difficult for women to understand if they have always perceived themselves as victims. They will say, "But I did stand up to my husband, and he hit me harder. What am I to do? He is stronger than I am." Understanding this lesson is what separates a weak woman from a strong woman … a victim from a victor.

Why do some women continually make bad choices for their lives, and other women seem to sail through life and not encounter the same heartaches and problems? I believe, from working with thousands of women over the years, that it is a matter of how you look at yourself as a child of God. Are you masochistic in your choices? Do you confront a problem the minute its ugly head appears, or do you choose to ignore it and hope it goes away? A truly liberated woman never places herself in situations where her self-respect and nobility of spirit will be compromised. I wish all mothers knew how to teach and reinforce this lesson with their daughters. A victor does not believe the lie that she is really "the problem" if she is abused in a marriage relationship; she will see the abuse for what it is and not tolerate it.

If you are a victim of abuse and are reading this book, do not condemn yourself because you have been blind to some of the realities of your situation. Instead, *starting today*, make decisions for yourself and your children that are healthy. You don't have to spend the rest of your life feeling that you are waste material being flushed down a toilet. God created a beautiful, splendid human being when He made you.

Choose not to be a victim. Choose to live healthier by making decisions that will make your future healthier. Choose your relationships as if you are a queen … a crown jewel … because you are one! The Lord thinks of you that way! You are not a lump of flesh and bone to be kicked, punched, and verbally assaulted. A change in mind-set about how you view yourself is a huge step toward living a healthier adult life. Do you want to be in an emotional hole the rest of your life? Do you want to continue to try to win the

approval of a spouse who thinks you are the problem, and the solution is his knuckles in your face?

Scripture does not condemn separation from an intolerable marital situation. God will provide the wisdom you need to come to terms with what you have to do to salvage your life, minute by minute, if you ask Him. Remember, you are a precious daughter who is incredibly loved by your heavenly Father. Claim that! Choose to live that way! The answers will come.

One type of victimization is not a result of ill-treatment by a spouse or other people. I think it is the most difficult to understand and cope with because it is "victimization by circumstances." What if you are dirt poor and see no way out of your desperate financial situation? What if you are hopelessly obese, and no diet in the world will take off the several hundred excess pounds you carry around every day as you listen to the whispers in the supermarket or the snickering when a chair crushes beneath you in a restaurant? What if you were born with a handicap that makes friendships difficult? Or a set of facial features that will always condemn you to the ranks of the unattractive in a society that is consumed with outward beauty?

This is the ultimate victimization because these things can't be blamed on anyone else. Since there is no one on whom to project the anger, it is turned inward. Women like this hate themselves. They find it almost impossible to understand how precious they are in the eyes of Jesus. They do not feel lovable, so it is incredibly difficult for them to experience the unlimited love that flows from Christ to His creation. However, once they comprehend this mystery, these women are the most wonderful witnesses for the gospel message; it dramatically changes their lives.

You may be one of these women. Whatever you do, don't make your pain as a victim the story in which you are stalled for the rest of your life. Do you know someone, perhaps a woman who has an appointment in the beauty shop the same time you do every

month, who has told the same sad tale over and over again for years? Everyone knows by heart about the dirty rotten bum she married, the unfair treatment she received in the divorce settlement, the endless custody problems. Many women never get beyond the one point in their life where they were hurt, and that becomes their life story. The difference between being a victor or a victim is getting beyond the pain and redefining how you will live your life.

There is a doctrine in counseling called the replacement principle. Counselors use this principle when they try to help someone who is "stuck" on a painful experience in their life that they cannot, or will not, release. The object is to stop focusing on the pain—to get "unstuck"—and leave the bitterness and resentment behind. Pain is part of the human condition; every single person who has lived on this planet has experienced pain of some sort in his or her life. Philippians 4:8 is God's "replacement principle":

> Finally, brethren, whatever is true, whatever is honorable, whatever is right, whatever is pure, whatever is lovely, whatever is of good repute, if there is any excellence and if anything worthy of praise, dwell on these things.

A counselor will use "catharsis" to eliminate a painful problem by bringing it to consciousness and affording it expression. A Christian uses this same principle through "confession," releasing the pain in prayer to our all-powerful God. A victim must release the marriage, her agony at failure, her anger at her spouse, her unfulfilled dreams, and place these things at the feet of Christ. If this is done successfully, she becomes a victor and can move on with her life. If unsuccessful, she takes back the problems and is not able to go on with her life in a healthy way. She remains a victim.

I know that many women reading this chapter will believe that I have a heart made out of brick. Actually, I'm a soft touch. However, I have little sympathy for women who remain victims, or

use the victim mentality to get their way at work and at home. I keep waiting to hear feminists say that genuine heroines are those who rise out of the mire of their existence and become the type of people we can really admire: women who get on with their lives because they aren't permanently stalled on their pain; women who take responsibility for their choices, who own their bad decisions, like my friends who admitted *they* made lousy selections when they married their husbands.

Women who are victims are always concerned about their needs. They tend to see things negatively; there is a huge hole in their "value bucket." They need constant reassurance. They cannot forgive the past, and it haunts their present. A heroic woman is one who gets past the pain, learns from that suffering, and gets on with her life.

There is a cliché that Christians use, perhaps overuse: "victory through Christ." However, it is a good phrase to remember whether or not you lean toward having a victim mentality. Romans 8:28 states that in all things God works for the good for those who love Him, and it couldn't be more clear that He will salvage your life, no matter what the mess, if you let Him. It is pretty hard to think of yourself as a helpless target of other people's unhealthy behavior if you claim that verse. God is the High Road. Choose Him! Galatians 5:22 reminds us that the fruits of the Spirit include self-control. When you take the high road at your place of work and in your relationships with others, you are released from the debilitating grasp of self-pity.

What does the future hold? Who will be the next set of victims that the feminists want to "fix"? The current power struggle for the feminists is ... guess what ... back to ground zero: the home. For the first time in decades, their spokeswomen are coming out for homemakers! They have had to; women have forced them to! Gene Edward Veith writes about the phenomenon of bright college women wanting to return to the role of homemaker:

Ironically, the idea that girls do so well in school does not fit well with the feminist agenda, which requires that women be seen as the hapless and helpless victims of the vast male conspiracy. Strong women—particularly those who show their strength in traditional social roles—get in the way of the theory. . . . Historically, powerful women in politics—from Elizabeth I and Queen Victoria through Margaret Thatcher—tend to be socially conservative, promoting the particular vocations of wives and mothers. So are many of the bright schoolgirls, who later discover that raising a family demands far more brains and creativity than they would need in the corporate world.[6]

This is going to get ugly. Feminists want to politicize the home just as they have politicized the workplace. They want equality for housewives in economic terms, and they want government regulations in place to see that this happens. In actuality, they view women very unkindly: They are either producers or parasites. To justify a woman having the gumption to stay at home to raise her children means that they have to make her into a producer, and producers get paid wages.

Do you understand where this thought line is going? If you are a homemaker and raising the next generation of children, do you consider yourself a parasite? A victim? That's what feminists think you are! Every homemaker in America should be insulted, and yet a part of me knows this emotion probably won't happen. Greed will win the day.

chapter 10

Final
Thoughts

Feminism as a worldview has wreaked havoc on our culture. Women aren't the only ones who have been warped by the movement. It has had a crippling effect on an entire generation of young men, who haven't a clue about how to relate to a woman in a healthy way. Millions of babies have been aborted as a result of "sexual freedom." Legions of abandoned, single moms are living at the poverty level, trying to make sense of their lives. Young boys have access to pornography on the Internet and are viewing material that will forever impact the way they relate to the women who will become their girlfriends, and maybe their wives. We live in a culture that appears sophisticated and affluent on the outside, but is in actuality, rotten at the core.

Where do we go from here?

A growing movement among the clergy maintains that spiritual revival is the only answer to fill the moral vacuum in our culture. It is emotionally painful for me to look back at the incredible women's movement we were bequeathed by Frances Willard, and see what our generation did to it. For every problem we thought we were solving, we created another, far more difficult to fix. How do we turn it around? What is the role of Christian women in the new millennium? Is revival the only answer?

For starters, I believe every woman needs to ask herself this question: Who in this life loves me, and whom do I love in return? *Whom* we love usually translates into *how* we spend our time. Sadly, for many women in our materialistic society, the question could more easily be answered if it were worded differently, and the *whom* was replaced by *what* ... what do I love?

If you are a Christian, hopefully your first response will be, "God loves me, and I love Him in return with all my heart, soul, mind, and strength." If this isn't your answer, it is a good starting point for how to respond to the lies that our culture has foisted on you as a female. God has to be the source of your self-esteem and how you view yourself as a woman. Looking to another human being, or to a cultural movement like feminism, for your inner peace and sense of worth will *always* result in disappointment. Your Creator God wants to have a personal relationship with you. He wants to be in communication with you daily. And He wants to give you the wisdom and direction that you need to have your life make sense in a culture gone crazy. There is no time like *right now*—this very minute—to recommit yourself to your relationship with your Savior.

If you are a daughter, wife, mother, or a woman with no husband or children, your response to the question might be that you have loved your parents, your husband, or your children in this lifetime, and in return, they have loved you. Or have they? What is your personal legacy for the people who have walked across the pages of your life history?

I was at Los Angeles International Airport recently waiting curbside for my husband. An elderly woman was standing close to me. She was the classic "Mom from Mayberry," and she sported a fresh perm, pearls, housedress, and very sensible shoes. She was clutching her handbag and bending from her waist toward the street, fretting over every car that passed, looking for someone special.

In the meantime, a very colorful character, indigenous to Hollywood, came to stand beside us. This young lady was tattooed over every square inch of her body except her face. She was wearing short shorts, a bikini top, high heels, and sported pink hair that progressed from pale pink at her forehead to purple at her neck. In addition, she was smoking two cigarettes. When she would remove one from her mouth with one hand, the other hand rammed in the second cigarette to take its place.

The little, round mother became very frightened by this apparition, and within minutes had sidled so close to me that I was actually holding her up. There were tears in her eyes, and she told me that she hoped her son hadn't forgotten her. Soon after, a car screeched to the curb, and a huge burly man who looked like a lumberjack got out, ran to his little mother, picked her up and twirled her around and around, to the delight of all of us watching. I saw the mother's face go from anxiety to fear to absolute joy within a matter of five minutes. And I will never forget the look on her son's face ... *unconditional* love for the mother he held in his arms.

That is the kind of love all of us would like to experience from our husbands, children, friends, and others the Lord brings into our lives. We all yearn for people to be genuinely thankful that we are a part of their existence. It's human nature to want that affirmation. And we all have the same number of hours in a day to give love, in return, to those who care for us. Are we using the hours in our day in the best possible way ... a way that honors our God and gives, as well as returns, the love that we have received from those around us? Do we act out daily the two commandments that Jesus said were *"the foremost"*? "And you shall love the Lord your God with all your heart, and with all your soul, and with all your mind, and with all your strength. The second is this, You shall love your neighbor as yourself. There is no other commandment greater than these" (Mark 12:30-31).

Time passes so very quickly. When we are young, we think that we have forever to accomplish the things we want to do with our lives. The older we get, we come to the awful realization that we really don't have that much time at all to make an impact for the Kingdom and to impart what is important to our families. What is our legacy to be? Will we be remembered as a sweet fragrance or as a noxious odor?

When my daughters were one and six years of age, I was in the grocery store shopping for the goodies for my oldest daughter's birthday party. She was so excited that she was running around the cart in circles. Her baby sister kept twisting in the safety seat, trying to grab anything she could out of the cart. It was late afternoon, and I was tired and becoming a little exasperated.

An elderly man was behind us in line, smiling benignly. He complimented me for having such charming daughters, and then he said with a touch of sadness, "Enjoy every moment with those precious children because in a blink of an eye, they're gone." I thought to myself, "Yeah, sure! You don't have to put up with all this every day!" Eighteen years later, we dropped our daughter off at college, and I cried the entire flight home over the loss of our children's daily presence in our lives. I remembered what the man had said to me in the store, and I acknowledged in my heart that he was absolutely right. In a blink of an eye, my children were gone.

I came home to an empty house, and the only things left were the memories of ballet lessons, dirty athletic gear, proms, camping trips, and family meal times ... all memories I cherished. I thought forward to a time when my children would come home to this same empty house, but I would be the one who was gone. What part of me would be stored in their memory banks? What remembrances would they cherish?

Edith Schaeffer writes in *What Is a Family?*,

> Memories not chosen, but given day by day, are also being collected. Is a slap in the face the first memory? Or is it the memory of Mommy still being there when the early streaks of dawn starting to come in through the curtains startle you into seeing that "Mommy has been up all night because I had the croup. She didn't go to bed at all. Oh, Mommy!" You can't choose the first memory; you

can't regulate what will be remembered and what will be forgotten. If there are enough lovely memories, and if there are apologies for making really wrong choices, then the museum will have a good balance and a non-romantic reality of what life is like.[1]

The Christian life is one of hard work and self-sacrifice. Selfishness and laziness have no part of it. That is what makes it so very difficult. It runs contrary to our human natures. It is contrary to postmodernism. It is contrary to the message of the feminist movement. One of our Focus board members is a dentist who often leads teams of medical personnel into third-world countries to spend weeks giving much-needed treatment to long lines of refugees. He is often asked, "How long do you work every day when you are on one of these medical missions?" His response is, "We don't measure our time by clocks or hours; we work *from can to can't.*"

A gentleman on the staff at Focus has taught his children that every person lives with one of two types of pain in his or her life, either the pain of discipline or the pain of regret. His favorite line is, "Pick your pain." Every woman has to make the same decision about how she will live her life: She has to pick her pain.

The irony of the feminist dogma is that it has eliminated choice in the lives of women, even though it is known by its "pro-choice" lingo. Women choose their pain by following a set of prescribed, politically correct choices that are supposed to guarantee personal happiness. But so much of the agenda results in direct pain and regret: The choice of reproductive freedom results in loss of human life; the choice of a professional career results in disappointments that could have been avoided if being a stay-at-home mom had been an honorable career choice; the choice of living together results in the loss of a long-term relationship based on the promises inherent in marriage.

- The feminists say that to be happy, you have to hate men. Yet God made men and women in His image (Genesis 1:27) with specific roles and attributes that show who He is to His creation. Each gender has incredible value in His sight.
- Feminists say that women should be freed from the responsibilities of caring for children, yet God created woman as the bearer and nurturer of children.
- Feminists say women have the right to kill their babies. God says He knows every baby even before they were formed in the womb, and they are precious to Him.
- Feminists say that the only way to be truly feminine is to be lesbian. Yet God says that the great love story He created is between a man and a woman, and not between two women.
- Feminists say that women are victims of male oppression, yet God views His noble daughters as worthy of male protection ... to the point of death. He illustrated this Himself, by willingly shedding His own blood for them on a wooden cross.

Pick your pain.

We are all faced with choices: Will we respond with love and blessings? Will we be a source of peace and protection for others who are being assaulted by the storms of this life? Will we put others before ourselves always? Will we be remembered for our selfless life . . . or as a canker sore? A giver or a taker? Will we be able to say, as the apostle Paul did in 2 Timothy 4:7-8,

> I have fought the good fight, I have finished the course, I have kept the faith. In the future there is laid up for me the crown of righteousness, which the Lord, the righteous Judge, will award to me on that day; and not only to me, but also to all who have loved His appearing.

Will we have kept the faith despite the cultural messages that bombard us that are contrary to what the Lord would have us be as Christian women? Can we be the opposite of this selfish generation? Can we impart that same selflessness to our children?

The great mystery that the feminists have never understood is that liberation does not come from equal opportunity in the workplace, nor from a college education, nor from possessing many materialistic toys, nor in having the perfect marriage, nor in being a mother. Those things bring us happiness, but meaning in life has another source. It doesn't come from any of those things. It comes only from having a personal relationship with Jesus Christ.

Correcting injustice may offer a societal "fix" to our many problems, inequality being one of them, but human nature has remained basically the same since Creation. The only true freedom, for men as well as women, is when they understand how precious they are in the eyes of an almighty heavenly Father, who became human flesh so we could know Him, and who died for us so that we could live with Him forever. A relationship with Him is the answer men and women have been aching for to fill the hunger and replace the anger in their lives. Yet they are too stubborn to say a prayer in the quiet of their room: "Lord, I want to know You. Reveal Yourself to me."

One of my closest friends prayed that prayer. But first, she left high school without a diploma. She had a voracious appetite for drugs and sex and had spent her youth in random entanglements with various men who meant nothing to her. She had an abortion. She married because she had to; her boyfriend of the month wanted the baby. One day, in suicidal despair, she said to the ceiling, "God, I have hit rock bottom. If You are real, You'll have to let me see You, because I'm dying."

The Lord not only revealed Himself to her in an incredible way, but also to her husband. They are now the parents of four children, and although she has been married for a dozen years, they are in reality still on their honeymoon. God is still in the miracle business, and He cares about *you* as much as He cares about this woman.

I have come to the conclusion that nothing in my life matters outside of my walk with the Lord and imparting the message of the gospel to my children and loved ones. It is a source of incredible comfort that my daughters are deeply committed Christians. However, close female friends and family members are not, and this separation from their Christian heritage happened within one generation. Cultural mouthpieces have indoctrinated these women with the feminist ideology throughout their lives, but it offers nothing except the bankruptcy of their souls. Feminists in their arrogance have replaced the sovereignty of God with the sovereignty of women. God has been rationalized out of existence.

This is the battle for Christian women today, and it is difficult, frustrating, and agonizingly painful: to impart the truth of the gospel to those who feel they have no need of it. God go with each of you as you fulfill His call on your life! Remember, the battle belongs to the Lord. *You* are an invaluable soldier in His army, and He will place you on the front lines if you volunteer for active duty! I challenge each of you to say, "I'm here, Lord. Use me!"

I'll see you on the battle front!

11. "Women Who Abort: Their Reflections on the Unborn," *Post-Abortion Review*, The Elliot Institute, Winter 1996, p. 1.
12. As quoted by Charles Carroll.
13. David Mastio, "Abortion Battles: More in Common Than We Think," *USA Today*, August 14, 1996, p. 17A.
14. "Clinton Signs Bill Allowing Research with Fetal Tissue," *St. Louis Post-Dispatch*, June 12, 1993, p. 4B.
15. Lynn Vincent, "The Harvest of Abortion," *World*, October 23, 1999, p. 16.
16. Ibid.
17. Richard Ostling, "Women Have Greater Acceptance of Religious Activism in Politics, Poll Notes," *Associated Press*, January 27, 1999.
18. Table 373: "Child Abuse and Neglect Cases Substantiated and Indicated—Victim Characteristics: 1990-1996," *Statistical Abstract of the United States,* 1998, p. 227.
19. Robert J. Samuelson, "Do We Care About Truth?" *Newsweek,* September 6, 1999, p. 76.
20. Achtemeier, "Abortion and the Sacraments."

Chapter 5

1. Amy Tracy, "A Relentless Pursuit," *Focus on the Family,* March 1998, p. 3.
2. Vincent, "The Harvest," p. 15.
3. Justin Torres, "Lesbian Summit Calls for New Brand of Gay Activism," *CNSNews.com,* April 27, 1999, see http://www.conservativenews.org.
4. Janet and Craig Parshall, *Tough Faith: Trusting God in Troubled Times* (Eugene, OR: Harvest House Publishers, 1999), p. 72.

Notes

Chapter 1

1. Diane Wagner, "Equal Rights Backers March for Amendment," *New York Times*, August 23, 1981, p. 29.
2. Lynn Vincent, "Worse Now Than Ever," *World*, July 24, 1999, p.14.

Chapter 2

1. Faith Martin, "Frances Willard: America's Forgotten Feminist," see http://www.springvalleypress.com/articles/f.willard.html.
2. Dana L. Robert, "In Stained Glass: Frances Willard and the Temperance Movement," http://www.bu.edu/ chapel/Chapel Webpages/temperance.html. Site no longer available.
3. Martin, "Frances Willard."
4. Robert, "In Stained Glass."
5. Martin, "Frances Willard."
6. Ibid.
7. Ibid.
8. Address of Frances E. Willard, President of the Women's National Council of the United States, Washington, D.C., February 22-25, 1891, see http://www.cohums. ohio–state.edu/history/courses/hist563/willard.html.
9. George T. B. Davis, The Greatest American Woman: Miss Frances E. Willard's Last Autographical Interview. Her Account of Her Methods of Work and Daily Life. Her Interpretation of Gospel Messages, see http://www. history. ohio-state.edu/projects/prohibition/willard/willard_last_interview.html.

10. Ibid.
11. Robert, "In Stained Glass."

Chapter 3

1. Liz Smith, "A Heart of Goldie," *Good Housekeeping*, April 1999, p. 125.
2. Ibid.
3. Ibid., p. 200.
4. Alanna Nash, "Solid Goldie," *Good Housekeeping*, July 1997, p. 76.
5. Smith, "A Heart of Goldie."
6. Francis Schaeffer, *How Should We Then Live?* (Old Tappan, NJ: Fleming H. Revell, 1976), p. 145.
7. "No Safe Place: Violence Against Women. An interview with Gloria Steinem," KUED-TV, Salt Lake City, UT, see http://www.media.utah.edu/prdction/interv/steinem.html.
8. Barbara Ehrenreich, "The Real Truth About the Female Body," *TIME*, March 8, 1999, pp. 61-65.
9. Jim Abrams, "Hill, Steinem Say Incident Is Not Harassment," *Associated Press*, March 23, 1998.
10. Jim Taylor, *Comedy and Tragedy* (Herndon, VA: Young America's Foundation, 1997).
11. Louise Silverstein and Carl Auerbach, "Deconstructing the Essential Father," *American Psychologist*, June 1999, Volume 54, No. 6., pp. 397-407.
12. Cal Thomas, "Parsing the Presidential Denial; Supporters Using the Usual Defenses," *Washington Times*, March 1, 1999, p. A15.
13. Gloria Steinem, *Revolution from Within: A Book of Self-Esteem* (New York: Little, Brown and Company, 1993), p. 259.
14. Marilyn French, *The Women's Room* (New York: Simon and Schuster, 1989).

15. Vincent, "Worse Now."
16. Abrams, "Hill, Steinem."
17. Tod Linberg, "Dreaming of Being Like Monica," *Washington Times*, July 8, 1998, p. A19.
18. Deborah Zabarenko, "Feminists Outraged by Impeachment Push," *Reuters*, December 15, 1998.
19. "Hillary Rodham Clinton Discusses Allegations Against Her Husband, Child Care, and the State of the Union Address," *Today*, January 27, 1998.

Chapter 4

1. Elizabeth Achtemeier, "Abortion and the Sacraments," *Theology Matters*, May/June 1999, p. 2.
2. Shulamith Firestone, *The Dialectic of Sex* (New York: Wm. Morrow & Co., 1970), p. 226.
3. Carol Everett, *The Scarlet Lady* (Brentwood, TN: Wolgemuth & Hyatt, 1991), p. 213.
4. Ravi Zacharias, *A Shattered Visage* (Grand Rapids, MI: Baker Book House, 1990), p.180.
5. "Can America Avoid the Mistakes of History?" *Focus on the Family Citizen*, October 20, 1997, p. 14.
6. Charles Carroll, "Nuremberg: Judgment and Challenge, The Rediscovery of the Law Above the Statutory," *United States Air Force Journal of Legal Studies*, Volume 6, 1995-1996 (USAFA Department of Law), p. 209.
7. William J. Federer, *America's God and Country Encyclopedia of Quotations* (Coppell, TX: FAME Publishing, Inc., 1994), p. 10.
8. Carroll, "Nuremberg."
9. "Eminent Theologian Points Toward Reformed Understanding of Unborn," *Presbyterians Pro-Life News*, Fall 1999, p. 1.
10. Ibid.

5. Hank Hanegraaff, *The Face That Demonstrates the Farce of Evolution* (Nashville, TN: Word Publishing, 1998), p. 24.

6. Ibid.

7. Fred Barnes, "Soccer Aside, Women Are (Still) Not Men," *Boundless*, August 6, 1999, see http://www.boundless.org/contents_main.html.

8. Charles Darwin, *The Descent of Man*, Great Books of the Western World, vol. 49, *Darwin*, edited by Robert Maynard Hutchins (Chicago: Encyclopedia Britannica, 1952), p. 566.

9. "Defending the Truth," *Focus on the Family* daily broadcast, July 13-15, 1999.

10. Bill Roundy, "Was Abraham Lincoln Gay?" *Washington Blade*, May 28, 1999.

11. Starla Allen and Patricia Allan, "Understanding the Roots of Lesbianism: Common Factors in the Lives of Women with Same-Sex Struggles" (Seattle, WA: Exodus International, 1997).

12. For more information on the Love Won Out conferences, please call Focus on the Family at 1-800-A-FAMILY (1-800-232-6459).

13. John and Anne Paulk, *Love Won Out* (Wheaton, IL: Tyndale House Publishers, 1999).

Chapter 6

1. Joyce Madelon Winslow, "Is Life Really Just the End of the Line?" *USA Today*, October 13, 1999, p. 17A.

2. Dewey Cornell, et al, "Characteristics of Adolescents Charged with Homicide," *Behavioral Science and the Law* 5 (1987), pp. 11-23.

3. "The Impact of Father Absence and Family Breakdown on Children's Educational Attainment," *In Focus*, Family Research Council, July 1993.

4. Ibid.
5. "Father Facts," The National Fatherhood Initiative, Gaithersburg, MD, p. 72.
6. Julia Duin, "'Real Men' Staying Away from Church, Author Says," *Washington Times*, September 27, 1999.
7. "The Early Documents," *The Feminist Chronicles*, Part IIIa, see http://www.feminist.org/research/chronicles/early1.html.
8. Ibid.
9. Suzanne Fields, "Zero-Sum Mating," *Washington Times*, July 26, 1999, p. A19.
10. Danielle Crittenden, *What Our Mothers Didn't Tell Us: Why Happiness Eludes the Modern Woman* (New York: Simon and Schuster, 1999).
11. Danielle Crittenden, "The Cost of Delaying Marriage," *Boundless*, May 1999.
12. Suzanne Fields, "Play, Boys," *Washington Times*, October 18, 1999, p. A19.
13. LaVonne Neff, "*Christianity Today* Talks to George Gilder" and "Civilizing the Sexual Barbarians," *Christianity Today*, March 6, 1987, p. 35.

Chapter 7

1. Hilary Alexander, "The High Street Evangelista: She's the Supermodel More Used to Haute Couture than St. Michael," *London Daily Telegraph*, August 13, 1992, p. 11.
2. Nash, "Solid Goldie," p. 76.

Chapter 8

1. Leon A. Danco, *Inside the Family Business* (Alfred, NY: The Center for Family Business, 1982).
2. NICHO Early Child Care Network, "Child Care and Mother-Child Interaction in the First 3 Years of Life," *Developmental Psychology*, Vol. 35, No. 6, November 1999, pp. 1399-1413.

Chapter 9

1. Susan Isaacs, *Brave Dames and Wimpettes* (New York: The Ballantine Publishing Group, 1999), p. 2.
2. Ibid., p. 5.
3. Joyce Howard Price, "Feminist Author Assails Peers for 'Heterophobia'; Sees Anti-Male Bias in Harassment Laws," *Washington Times,* November 8, 1999, p. A1.
4. Nancy Gibbs, "When Is It Rape?" *Time,* June 3, 1991, p. 52.
5. "Success and Significance Survey Results of Women in Leadership," presentation given by Priority Associates, Spring 1999.
6. Gene Edward Veith, "Feminist Misogyny," *World,* January 9, 1999, p. 6.

Chapter 10

1. Edith Schaeffer, *What Is a Family?* (Grand Rapids, MI: Baker Book House, 1975), p. 173.

Other Faith and Family Strengtheners
From Focus on the Family ®

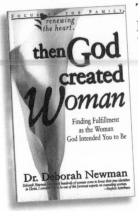

Then God Created Woman

It's a simple fact: women are relational beings. Yet when it's intimacy we crave, we often turn to those who simply cannot fulfill our expectations. Realizing this, author and psychologist Deborah Newman takes readers back to the Garden of Eden to identify all women's deepest need—a close, intimate relationship with the Lord. For only when we wholly rely on God will we find freedom as the beautiful, confident creations He intended us to be: reflections of Himself. Paperback.

Renewed Hearts, Changed Lives

They came carrying heavy burdens—an unfaithful husband, a struggle with infertility, family problems. But when they left, they were different women, met by a faithful God. Read the amazing personal accounts, written by Betsy Holt with commentary by Lisa Harper, of women who found hope and healing after attending a Focus on the Family *Renewing the Heart* conference. Paperback.

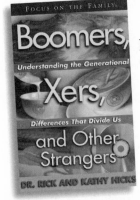

Boomers, Xers, and Other Strangers

Ever wondered why people seem so different in their values, lifestyles and opinions? Chances are, it's because of how they saw the world while growing up. An entertaining and informative look at how each generation was shaped. Authors Dr. Rick and Kathy Hicks also help us understand how our values often differ—and why. Paperback.

•   •   •

Look for these special books in your Christian bookstore or request a copy by calling 1-800-A-FAMILY (1-800-232-6459). Friends in Canada may write Focus on the Family, P.O. Box 9800, Stn. Terminal, Vancouver, B.C. V6B 4G3 or call 1-800-661-9800.

Visit our Web site (www.family.org) to learn more about Focus on the Family or to find out if there is an associate office in your country.

FOCUS ON THE FAMILY®

$\mathcal{W}$elcome to the $\mathcal{F}$amily!

Whether you received this book as a gift, borrowed it from
a friend, or purchased it yourself, we're glad you read it! It's just
one of the many helpful, insightful and encouraging
resources produced by Focus on the Family.

In fact, that's what Focus on the Family is all about—providing inspiration, information and biblically based advice to people in all stages of life.

It began in 1977 with the vision of one man, Dr. James Dobson, a licensed
psychologist and author of 16 best-selling books on marriage, parenting,
and family. Alarmed by the societal, political, and economic pressures
that were threatening the existence of the American family, Dr. Dobson
founded Focus on the Family with one employee—an assistant—
and a once-a-week radio broadcast, aired on only 36 stations.

Now an international organization, Focus on the Family is dedicated
to preserving Judeo-Christian values and strengthening the family
through more than 70 different ministries, including eight separate
daily radio broadcasts; television public service announcements;
11 publications; and a steady series of books and award-winning
films and videos for people of all ages and interests.

Recognizing the needs of, as well as the sacrifices and important
contribution made by, such diverse groups as educators, physicians,
attorneys, crisis pregnancy center staff and single parents,
Focus on the Family offers specific outreaches to uphold and
minister to these individuals, too. And it's all done for one purpose,
and one purpose only: to encourage and strengthen individuals
and families through the life-changing message of Jesus Christ.

• • •

For more information about the ministry, or if we can be of help to your
family, simply write to Focus on the Family, Colorado Springs, CO 80995
or call 1-800-A-FAMILY (1-800-232-6459). Friends in Canada may write
Focus on the Family, P.O. Box 9800, Stn. Terminal, Vancouver, B.C. V6B 4G3
or call 1-800-661-9800. Visit our Web site—www.family.org—
to learn more about Focus on the Family or to find out if
there is an associate office in your country.

We'd love to hear from you!